I0802388

COACHING YOUNG COUCH POTATOES

COACHING YOUNG COUCH POTATOES

A GAME PLAN FOR RAISING *RESPONSIBLE* YOUNG ADULTS

MICHAEL CLAPIER

PLAIN SIGHT PUBLISHING

An Imprint of Cedar Fort, Inc.
Springville, Utah

ISBN 13: 978-1-4621-2081-9

Published by Plain Sight Publishing, an imprint of Cedar Fort, Inc., 2373 W. 700 S., Springville, UT 84663
Distributed by Cedar Fort, Inc., www.cedarfort.com

LIBRARY OF CONGRESS CONTROL NUMBER: 2017938752

Cover design by Priscilla Chaves
Cover design © 2017 by Cedar Fort, Inc.
Edited and Typeset by Kimiko Christensen Hammari

Printed in the United States of America

10 9 8 7 6 5 4 3 2 1

Printed on acid-free paper

Thank you, Linda, for teaching me
how to give to our children,
for your belief in this book, and
for your ever present camera.

Coaching is an art form, a process of mentoring young people through a critically important and personal time. Two important results occur when you do coaching right: kids have fond memories that you created for them, and they continue to enjoy physical activity for the rest of their lives.

Raising a responsible child is the crowning achievement of effective parenting and quality coaching. In a world where raising responsible children is a challenge, the time spent in youth sports may be one of our best opportunities to fully develop children.

On a winter's day I walked by an unused baseball field.
I did not see an empty lot.
I saw a glorious canvas waiting for the coach to paint meaning,
confidence, and joy upon the souls of children at play.

—Michael Clapier

CONTENTS

INTRODUCTION

A New Coaching Paradigm

In a perfect world, everyone grows up healthy, wealthy, and strong. Each child loves to play. Parents never argue and happiness blesses us all. Unfortunately, the world we live in is less than perfect. We are challenged on all sides by the pull of economic need and the reality that childlike play is being dissolved by electronic fires that fill our children's eyes and time.

During the past twenty-five years, I have coached young athletes, endured the counsel of their parents, and puzzled over the ingredients that create effective coaching of kids. Two of my daughters have been full scholarship Division I NCAA runners. My son and sons-in-law have been Division I NCAA, NJCAA, NAIA athletes, USA Junior Olympic national champions, high school varsity athletes, and youth coaches.

I have coached undefeated high school wrestlers, state champions, varsity athletes, and league champions in football, softball, baseball, wrestling, track field, and cross country. During those years, my passion was trying to understand the mechanics of coaching and how to influence our children for the rest of their lives. I have questioned the ways in which we define success and work hard to serve the cause of youth sports as coaches, officials, and parents.

My qualifications for writing this book are the thousands of hours I have spent in the service of young people, continually testing and applying the things I learned into the pedagogy of what I teach. While carefully assessing the athletes while they struggle between success and failure through all levels of competition, I have learned much about how to coach young people.

In these pages, I reveal lessons learned that are not only important but also effective as you implement them into youth coaching programs. I know what I have seen, and I have seen skills and techniques that work and attitudes and actions that do not. I have seen coaches work wonders and others create disasters. I have seen kids cry, heard mothers complain, and watched officials shake their heads at both.

I believe there is a new way to consider how we coach today's young athletes. The impact of sedentary lifestyles and shortened attention spans challenges coaching like nothing before, not to mention disappearing respect for sportsmanship, fair play, and work. There is more benefit in teaching these concepts and strategies than winning games.

I will show you how to do that, and more. Responsible children are the by-product of effective youth coaching.

An Apparent Need

A doctor commits to first do no harm. Adults supervising children make no such commitment, but perhaps they should.

I was involved with Little League football for nearly ten years. We were part of a conference with about eight thousand participants from eight to fourteen years of age. The teams averaged twenty athletes. With two assistants and a head coach on each team, eight thousand boys and girls were in the care of twelve hundred coaches. The league offered no training to those coaches.

Once every three years, an active coach was required to attend a four-hour session in order to maintain sideline credentials. Most of those meetings consisted of an argument on what constituted cheating. A few procedural matters were discussed, but my impression of the three meetings I attended was that nothing mattered more than winning; athletes were merely working parts of personal winning machines. I was offered no tips on coaching, other than a brief discussion on heatstroke and a conversation on concussions, but only because I asked questions.

The stubborn arrogance of coaches was discouraging because it was supported by a league that saw no need to improve coaching skills. I helped with teams that my own boys were on and usually served as the trainer. I liked this role because I could help kids individually and did not have to deal with coaches, their politics, or bad practice. My ideas were originally rejected by these know-it-all coaches. In time, however, coaches noticed that my suggestions created improvement and strengthened performances. Eventually, others began adopting my philosophy and techniques to produce winning programs. The only championship teams produced within our Little League football district over the past ten years were coached by myself or coaches using the principles and techniques I developed.

Why Involve Yourself in Coaching at All?

For me, coaching has always been a grand excuse for spending time with my children. Watching from the stands has never been as enjoyable as pacing the sidelines, knowing the players, and experiencing the action of play and competition. I like this involvement and doubt that I am different from other coaches in that respect. I want children to have a good experience on my team and hope to justify coaching as time well spent with my own children and their friends.

When watching other coaches, I am fascinated, frustrated, and even angered by the huge number of disconnects that I see between them and their kids. As I became a student of Little League sports, my notes, case studies, and the results that I achieved by applying what I was learning formed the basis of this book. I created success by applying every principle, technique, and drill that I share in these pages.

Through wrestling, baseball, football, and track and field with my own children (and soccer, softball, swimming and lacrosse with their friends), I have noticed a change in the way that children learn, a difference in the responsibilities they are willing to accept regarding work, and varying levels of interest that they commit to sports.

Coaching Young Couch Potatoes is a collection of my observations and the skills, techniques, and procedures that I know work. I have used them in workouts and employed them during competition. I have seen them work for other coaches and know they will work for you as well. More important, now that I have the luxury of looking at my experience from the vantage of years gone by and young athletes grown older, I know that Little League is about much more than winning a game. It is about developing young people in a world where few of them want to grow.

Ours is a world that rejects personal responsibility. Even adults seek escape from obligation. Is it any wonder that we are challenged more than ever by the task of raising responsible children in an irresponsible world? Through the course of this book, I will share the lessons I have learned about coaching youth and setting them up for success for the rest of their lives.

What Was Then Is Not Now

In order to effectively coach today's young athletes, and subsequently raise responsible children, we must reconsider the ways in which we handle our present coaching assignments and, to a greater degree, our parenting skills. More often than not, they are one and the same. This book will effect positive change in your coaching experience as soon as your next workout.

If we used an electronics schematic for a 1952 television as our guide to repair a 48-inch plasma TV, we would have very little chance of successfully producing high-definition television. However, that is exactly what we do when we attempt to coach today's child with yesterday's opinions and no one's skills. I suggest it is time to stop coaching the way we were coached. It is time to recognize the environments that are producing our children and open our minds to new ways of coaching. I am proposing modifications that are necessary, essential, and long past due.

Children are different today than they were even ten years ago. The childhood of my children is very different from my own. As a child, I spent hours in the fields of our Idaho farm with no cell phone, Internet, DVD, or cable television. Because I was alone, I thought a lot and used my imagination. I watched battles with evil enemies in my head.

Children today battle evil through interactive video games in which visualization comes not from imagination but through technologies that entertain and ultimately rob creativity, personal experience, and healthy exercise. Tomorrow's child will be even more sedentary and even less prone to engage in physical exercise and ultimately accept responsibility for their own actions. Children process instruction differently. They experience life through a wider variety of personal and mediated experiences than we did. They do not play outdoors to the extent that any previous generation did.

Today, a child's involvement in sports is an addendum to their lifestyle rather than the mainstay. The workout is considered a distraction from other areas of interest affecting their performance, attendance, and attitude. When we fail to recognize the present needs of youth sports, we flirt with a dangerous precedent that might diminish a child's potential for the meaningful life experience that sports can give.

The realities surrounding our children as they participate in sports are shifting. Experienced coaches reluctantly accept change, and inexperienced coaches have neither bad habits nor offer good counsel. The art of coaching—and it truly is an art form when correctly employed—remains frozen in time between increasing societal trends affecting our children's behavior and old-school coaching mentalities that weld us to ineffective traditions.

What This Book Gives You

Little League coaches, hungry for ways of understanding behavior, personality, and physicality patterns, can immediately implement effective processes within their programs. These strategies are easy to understand and simple to use. Their effectiveness is only challenged by your willingness to openly consider these new paradigms. If you use them, they will help. As you master them, you will move your coaching to a powerful new level and give children a positive experience. You will also win more games.

Youth athletics, from their early years through middle school, set patterns for physical growth and establish habits for future exercise and health benefits. Successful coaching gives an intimate introduction and a positive experience into that physical activity. Good coaches create a capacity and momentum that lasts beyond Little League and affects children on a number of personal and professional levels.

High school athletes, and to a greater extent college athletes, are either naturally gifted or were fortunate to benefit from excellent Little League coaching. As a skilled coach, you can deliver kids to high school prepared for varsity competitive levels.

Unfortunately, if you are a poor Little League coach, you will accelerate the departure of young athletes from competitive sport and deprive them of opportunities to move up the ladder of improved physical skill.

In the worst case scenario, a bad experience will remove a child's interest in exercise completely. But if you become an exceptional coach, you affect the future of every child on your team.

I trust that you seek to make your interaction with your athletes positive, long-lasting, and life-changing. I believe you will find this book to be a trusted resource that supports you as you create a meaningful experience for your athletes, their parents, and yourself.

Good luck!

1

YOUNG ATHLETES TODAY ARE DIFFERENT THAN YOU WERE

Get Over It

My son was no athlete. The positive team experience and fitness goals that he accepted as part of the team inspired healthy eating. He made those decisions on his own, set goals, and began exercising every day. He took control of his own life in junior high school. Later he discovered a passion for cycling and recently graduated with a master's degree in Information Technology.

—*Kathryn J., Mother*

I'M AN IDAHO FARM BOY. I grew up in a country setting where physical activity was a way of life. There were always chores to do, animals to feed, crops to irrigate, and interesting places to play. We were seldom drawn indoors by television and never by video games or computers. When I was ten years old, I could throw a bale of hay and my brother off the haystack.

A huge stack of straw bales provided one of my most delightful memories of physical activity. My Grandpa George put a fresh crop of straw next to his corrals to use as bedding through the winter for his cows. He sent my cousin Stan and me to the top to throw bales down. We soon discovered that throwing each other off the pile was fun because landing in the straw was painless. The battle at the top was thrilling. (As I remember, Stan did most of the falling.) We spent an entire day climbing, fighting, and throwing each other down. It was fun. It was physical. We were exultant.

We knocked a lot of straw off Grandpa's stack. We changed the symmetry from square to round and tore the twine string from more bales of straw than we could repair. But lucky for us, Grandpa valued developing good boys more than maintaining a good-looking stack of straw. He loved us and understood the value of physical play.

I remember him often when I think of a coaching model. Even when our behavior varied from his expectations, he recognized the value of our play. He saw it reflecting in our eyes and let our fun guide his reaction to that activity. In other words, he did not get mad. He knew that our play served the greater good of growing young people, and he channeled our enthusiasm instead of resisting our exuberance or letting it bother him. He did, however, strongly suggest that we rebuild his straw stack. And we did, more than once.

Fast forward thirty years. We live in a very different world. The lack of physical activity in our children's sedentary lifestyles is reaching dangerous and epidemic levels powered by a vast wasteland of electronic time-fillers. Thinking young people know how to play a game, work, or use physical ability can be a dangerous expectation. Media and sedentary behaviors fill much and control most of children's leisure time, yet we immediately expect them to "play ball."

The State of Our Youth's Health

From 1980 to 2004, the number of overweight children ages six to eleven more than doubled from 7 percent to 18 percent of our population. During that same time, the number of overweight children ages twelve to nineteen more than tripled from 5 percent to 17.1 percent of our population.

Obesity is the excessive accumulation of body fat present when total body fat is more than 25 percent in boys and more than 32 percent in girls. Between 5 and 25 percent of children and teenagers in the United

States are obese. As many as one child in four is in physical danger from too little exercise and too much poor food.

These numbers are frightening. The problem belongs to us all, not just children. It is a problem that we, their parents, are handing them. Nearly 65 percent of America's adult population is overweight, and 33 percent are clinically obese, a number that has risen more than 30 percent during the past three decades. Childhood and teenage obesity has almost tripled in the last decade alone. Obesity is now one of the leading causes of death in America, second only to tobacco use.[1]

Lack of exercise is stealing the essence of health from our children. Consider the following statistics:

- Every hour children play video games or watch television may double their risk of obesity.
- In the United States, childhood obesity rates have tripled over the last twenty years.
- England is planning to create cities of 20,000 inhabitants specifically designed to combat obesity in children.

Video games successfully compete for young people's time at every age.

- Video game play is replacing children's physical activity.
- On average, eighth grade boys play video games twenty-three hours a week, and eighth grade girls play them twelve hours a week.
- Studies now indicate that electronic games should be limited to prevent childhood obesity.

Assume Nothing about Their Ability

Physicality is the body's ability to perform athletically and to move physically. It becomes a measurement of an individual's level of biomechanical capacity. The lack of this capacity is the single greatest threat to childhood development and health. Because declining levels of physical fitness, increasing choices for sedentary entertainment, and bad eating habits are producing children so vastly different from

1 "World Health Organization Fact Sheet Number 311," updated March 2011—August 18, 2011, http://www.who.int/mediacentre/factsheets/fs311/en/

those even a decade ago, your job as a coach becomes more important than ever before. You must deal with more than you might imagine.

As you delve into your role as youth coach, parent, or mentor, you may be the best hope that an athlete has for not only enjoying the game but also building a foundation of quality experience that will affect them the rest of their life. You may think that sounds like too much power and responsibility. But it is not. You stand at a powerful crossroad for every child in your care. Most parents want youth sports to provide an outlet for physical activity, counteract their children's lack of exercise, and allow them time to safely have fun. Not only must youth coaches teach the rules of the game, but we must also work with a growing number of children who lack even basic physical ability. It is through the potential of each child that we draw the power to continue in our role. The games may be played now, but the legacy of our coaching can last forever.

Let Each Beginning Be Simple

On the first day of a wrestling class, I let the kids run, jump, roll, vault, walk, skip, and do everything I can think of so I can watch them experience basic balance and movement. This is especially important if some kids are new to the sport. Regardless of the sport you are coaching, you must determine level one competence before moving to level two. I never assume that a child whom I have never coached brings any skill to their first day of practice. It is important to put them through these motion exercises. You must see how they move so that you know what you have to work with, where to start, and how to design your workouts.

No Physical Conditioning

Because so many youth are growing into maturity with little or no physicality, athletic trainers have developed a new phrase to describe this dangerous lifestyle. *De-conditioned* describes a person who has never been in shape and does nothing to contribute to a healthy physical condition. They live so far removed from physical activity that they lack even basic muscle tone. Without necessary encouragement and needed skills to change their lifestyle, their options become limited—get healthy or die.

Is it any wonder that coaching is more than showing up for practice in Little League? We must not only teach the growing generation to play the games but also learn to love exercise. We have a difficult job on our hands.

The Purpose Isn't What You Think

Youth sport programs give children a laboratory to investigate life's experience. Through youth sports, children develop more than physicality. They acquire social skills that allow them to work with others, experience the value of working toward a simple goal, learn the disappearing art of winning with class or losing with grace, and discover the importance of being active now and through the rest of their lives. No one disagrees that these are important issues. You, their coach, are the guardian of the gate, the keeper of the keys, the dispenser of wisdom and insight. A coach is not just the guy or gal who yells when things go wrong.

Coaching's Great Questions

Little League sports give children supervised activity in a safe environment. When winning becomes the paramount activity, then a number of grand paradoxes emerge:

- How do I win if my athletes can't play?
- How can I teach them to play when they have the attention span of mosquitoes?
- How do I help them physically work when their idea of work reflects neither effort nor physicality?

What Brings You to Coaching?

Someone decides to coach for one of two reasons: to spend time with their children or to prove something for themselves. The first group is larger, the second group more dangerous. I believe the two types of coaches can best be described as *wannabes* and *should-a-beens*.

Wannabes want to be good coaches, be involved in a quality experience for their own or other children, and be part of an organization that benefits their community. Winning a few games is a nice plus.

Should-a-beens should have been greater than they remember, should have had better high school or college careers, should have been professional athletes, and in a few cases, should have been more committed to the children than to controlling the outcome of the games.

Fortunately, most coaches fall into the first category. Good volunteer coaches act upon an opportunity to connect youth sports and healthy exercise to time spent with children. Even though their motives are good, they have little or no practical experience. Most of their coaching experience comes from playing sports in their youth.

Even with good personal memories, the value of previous experience is minimal, if valid at all. Both today's environment and children are so different from past generations that coaching is like nothing seen before. Most coaches want to do a good job and are willing to learn. Reading this book is evidence of your desire to gain skills to help young athletes.

Destructive coaches, the should-a-beens, are too proud and stuck in their ways to accept advice or counsel. They coach blindly, use outdated intuition, and overlook most of what is needed to effectively connect with and help children. Too many try to recapture something from their own youth, something that they failed to realize as a competitor, and end up as tyrants. They inject the worst of the coaching experience into the innocence of children's games.

Tyrannical coaches are created through a variety of situations. Perhaps they thought they were better athletes than they actually were, or they may believe that their own child is a better athlete than performance validates. They crave power, want to be in charge, or simply do not know better. They are often proud, which means they do not listen; stubborn, which means they will not change; defiant, which means they ignorantly use outdated methods. Whatever the reason, these should-a-been coaches are blind to the varying behaviors of children, the difference of time, and the culture in which they coach. They remain neither able to see what is nor envision what might be.

Trying to prove something through coaching often means that winning games is your only measurement of success. Should-a-beens fail to intelligently measure the cost of winning and are left out of balance. A good coach knows that winning is not the most important reason for involvement. The goal of coaching is not to prove anything. It is to help children.

If you win all of your games, does that prove you are the best? If you lose all your games, does that indicate that you are the worst? Not necessarily—and usually not at all!

Worst or Best of What?

Every win-at-all-cost program I have observed, including high school and college programs, reaches the championship levels by stepping over the bodies of injured children or by manipulating rules of conduct and eligibility in some manner. Creating injury as a result of your coaching can never justify a program. (College and professional athletics are not part of this discussion. They are entirely different animals representing entirely separate scenarios.) Little League sports, when conducted in their most positive format, are simply a game. Anything can happen during competition. The playing ground of youth sports is vastly different from higher levels of sport. The imbalance of talent and purpose is so diverse and the disparity of skills so vast that youth coaches must be careful not to put such import into conclusions such as "I win, therefore you are a loser." Winning and losing prove nothing. They are simply a measurement of the child's play. A child becoming a healthier person is too complex and the future's sake too important to impose such unweighted dichotomies of purpose as winning and losing on children's lives. A child on a losing team is not a loser, yet they can be labeled as such by their competitors, coaches, and themselves.

Coaches must never get caught up in labeling. They must empower growth. Children are growing, and they can become discouraged because of you. Better yet, they can be encouraged by you because you control the environment.

How Did You Become a Coach?

More often than not, coaches are picked by default. In my career, I have never heard an administrator ask a volunteer coach if they know how to teach, warm up and cool down, comprehend the techniques of physical skills, how to stretch muscles, or play by the official rules of the game. The conversation usually goes like this: "Are you willing to give the time?" When the volunteer says "yes," he or she becomes the coach.

However, first-time coaches usually have the best intentions and are most willing to enter the season for sportsmanship and fair play's sake. I love new coaches because they accept the challenge of coaching kids, claiming their only qualification is a desire to serve.

Every Dog Has to Learn New Tricks

I remember my first experience coaching baseball. I received the assignment because I wanted to spend time with my son. I thought I knew something about baseball. After all, I had been an All-Star twenty years before. I remembered my experience there, so how tough could it be?

During my first meeting, I sat slack-jawed as a more experienced coach explained the draft process to me. *Draft?* I thought. *With eight-year-olds? Are you kidding me?* He was not kidding, and I began learning when we conducted a draft. No one helped me understand what I was looking for while watching the athletes run, hit, and throw. I even asked for help and of course received none. Every coach I was going to compete against was happy to let me struggle. My only process for learning was to make mistakes. I made plenty so that you do not have to.

I rarely see a coach willing to share the secrets of his success. Many of the people I have coached with and against remain silent on issues of player capacity and workout structure. Why should they help me beat them? Because no one would share their secrets, I was left to discover for myself how to create a meaningful experience for my team.

May I make the following suggestions for your role as a coach of America's young couch potatoes? Create a positive experience, have fun, develop physical skills, keep the kids safe, exercise large muscles, expand their lungs and challenge their minds, teach them the rules of the game, show them sportsmanship, and deliver them at the end of the season eager for continuing experiences in sport.

If you volunteer your time to help young people, you are to be congratulated. It is your great blessing to help children develop the fundamentals of a sport, learn the lessons that sports offer, and create an environment where young athletes can enjoy meaningful exercise while overcoming the lack of physicality that their sedentary lifestyles creates.

The need for participation in youth sports is evident. Children require places and occasion to play. Unfortunately, the current condition of our world is at best a challenge and at worst disturbing. But if you remember that coaching kids is about them and not you, and are willing to begin rethinking this great opportunity, you can master this rewarding art form.

What is the return on your child's time spent in youth sports?

- 1 sport (you may be involved in more than one)
- 6 hours per practice
- 4 hours per week in competition
- 10-week season
- 41 million US kids
- 9.84 billion hours

Americans spend billions of hours every year engaging their children in youth sports. If your child plays a second sport, you can double those hours. What do they gain from this huge amount of time spent in play? Surely we want our children to have fun, learn to play in organized ways, and exercise their growing bodies. But what do children actually gain from Little League?

They gain one of two philosophies: how to win at all costs (and possibly hate exercise for the rest of their lives) or to love sports, work hard, and understand the value of responsibility. The difference in the quality of one child's experience over another's will always be found in the coach.

2

LESS TALKING, MORE WORKING

How to Avoid Coaching's Worst Mistake

> I'm a nerd. I love science, numbers, and their applications. Coach Mike taught me that I mattered as an athlete and that I could contribute to a team. I wrestled and ran distance and cross country. I learned to keep working even when I didn't understand which describes research. I hold degrees in physics and applied mathematics. I am a PhD candidate in astro physics.
>
> —*Trevor B., PhD Candidate*

I PARKED MY CAR AND headed across a local practice field, one of those wonderful grassy playgrounds that bless our lives with its availability and space. Several baseball and soccer teams were practicing there.

My son's Little League baseball team was starting its workout. I arrived late, hoping to watch the workout and run down a few baseballs so more boys could hit. I was not coaching this team. I was just happy to be a dad and enjoy the afternoon.

During my walk from park to practice, I noticed a soccer team on the field next to the baseball diamond. About twenty-five girls were furiously dribbling soccer balls. They looked to be about eleven or twelve years old, and they were having the time of their lives. Each girl had a ball. Each player was physically engaged, laughing, running, commenting on their struggles, and shrieking with joy at their flubs. They were totally involved in physicality and individual skills; move the ball, work the feet, set up a kick, and shoot on the goal.

I thought they had a great coach because they were richly engaged in the skills of soccer. Everyone had equal opportunity for exercise, they were having fun, and they were all working. My walk to the dugout only took about five or six minutes, and the soccer team was engaged in this drill the entire time. The coach soon dismissed them for a drink of water.

Meanwhile, I grabbed a glove and headed for the outfield to help with my son's workout. After running down a few hits, I looked across to the soccer practice and noticed that the coach had directed his athletes to sit on a line extending across the field; one line, twenty-five girls sitting, and no one speaking. I soon realized, at the coach's direction, there was to be no talking. At the first sign of conversation, the coach yelled.

"Sit down. Be quiet."

Coach was going to talk.

The glee was gone, the physical exercise removed.

This coach was about to commit the single worst mistake of Little League coaching: too much talking and not enough working.

For the next half hour, the coach fought the girls' desires to move, squelched their inclination to speak, and removed both elements of play and fun from his workout. While battling the girls' natural inclinations to move and play, he was attempting to be heard and understood. He believed he was improving the girls' ability to play soccer, but that wasn't happening.

We Have to Talk, Don't We?

While it is true that we must verbally communicate, talking too much and working too little is a disaster. I see coaches constantly make this mistake, and it makes me crazy. The job is not about you. The kids are not there for you. You are there for them as a mentor, friend, first-aid expert, parent, administrator, reconciler, visionary, and energetic teacher.

Coaching is the complex blending of these skills into a person guided by the best interests of those young athletes. Notice that I did not include winning or personal accomplishment in my list of a coach's roles. The aforementioned benefits of coaching derive their power to create change in the positive experience that defines your program, and it happens mostly through your skillful use of play.

What Is Play?

My grandson, Tate, is fourteen months old and is learning to walk. Watching him experience physical motion for the first time is captivating.

After dinner the other night, the kids were playing on the lawn. Tate was playing with a push toy. When it bumped up against the curb and no longer rolled, he pushed it until it fell over. He was not discouraged. There was no outcome assigned to the effort, only discovery. He was simply playing. When the toy was on its side, he explored that side. When he fell through the legs of the toy and landed upside down on his head, he kept moving until he rolled onto his other side. He turned to his stomach, pushed with his feet, emerged from the toy, stood up, and began again. No fuss, no discouragement, just motion and focus while discovering what his body could do and amusement as he interacted with the toy. I was watching the nature of play and thought of its parallels in coaching. Only a child at play will work this hard without judgment or discouragement.

A toddler mastering motion requires, in principle, the same process that you must put your athletes through while helping them master new physical skills for a specific sport. Even a task as simple as pushing a ball around the floor revealed principles required to coach young couch potatoes. When Tate pushed his toy, reached for it, watched it, and caught it as it moved, his muscles remembered his successes. For him it was play. For me, it was a revelation.

On first observation, this play was good. His mother was pleased because he was content. The family was grateful because he was quiet. On a deeper level, he was exploring the physicality of each moment and working his way through solutions to exercise puzzles. Each movement led to more movement, which built upon the previous level of competency. As each particular skill became second nature, he added new movement and grew in his ability to perform more complex physical motion.

Tate was able to play with the push toy, but because he could barely walk, asking him to jump rope would have been unthinkable. Yet how often do youth coaches demand more performance from their players than ability allows? We constantly want level six, eight, or ten performances from athletes with level two skills. Coaches expect running like deer from kids who labor at plodding like elephants. This is not to imply that young athletes are not gifted—many are—but regardless of the levels of skill and ability to play, every kid you coach can improve. Great coaching means that you work with, help, and improve each kid on your team. You empower all your athletes toward a greater level of physical motion, thus creating a positive Little League experience. Poor coaching pushes even the best players away from the love of a sport and pulls them toward the vacuum of inactivity.

While You Talk, They Are Not Playing

A great Little League coach never neglects the value of play and makes it the foundation of his coaching. Not only is it an ally for building skills, but play is also your partner for connecting athletes to the training tasks at hand. The number-one reason kids get involved in youth sports is to have fun. The number-one reason they leave a sport is it stops being fun.

Children stay in a particular sport an average of 2.6 years. The principal method for teaching skills and connecting athletes with their future is play. Youth coaches must never lose sight of the value of play. Sport is, after everything else, play. We play baseball and soccer. We watch professionals play football or basketball. The baseball umpire yells, "Play ball" to start the game. He does not say, "Begin shouting or cursing or wishing you are somewhere else." He says "play," and play is fun. I think we are losing sight of that. Do not let your program facilitate play's demise. The wise use of play empowers you as a coach to teach skills, grow competency, and develop athletes. Too much talking limits play.

Why Play Helps You Be a Better Coach

Play is the path around your athletes' lack of attention. For example, wrestlers need strong shoulders. They need to move across the mat on their hands and toes. Crawling agility, core muscle strength, and strong arms and shoulders are essential to the sport. The old-school way to build shoulder strength is push-ups. I would recommend that you engage in a new process regardless of the sport. I created a new workout that capitalized on my athletes' needs to play while building muscles in the same manner as push-ups.

One Solution

While coaching a junior high school wrestling team, I noticed that my athletes soon burned out on push-ups. It was hard work for all of them and painfully hard for the couch potatoes. It is common for junior high kids to be unable to do several push-ups, so I made a game.

I had my team form a weight line. They lined up from smallest to largest and then counted off by two to separate the athletes evenly. I put the "ones" on one side of the wrestling room and the "twos" on the other. I grabbed ten small towels, rolled them up, ran tape around them, and placed them evenly on a line across the middle of the mat. I then told the wrestlers that the game was to get to a towel, stay on hands and feet, move to the far wall, and hold the towel against it. If they did not get their hands on a towel, then they had to stop the opposing athletes who had grabbed a towel from reaching the wall behind them. They could wrestle, push the other guy around, steal the towel, throw it to a teammate, or take it to the wall.

I blew the whistle and the action began. They loved it. Pushing off the wall and scrambling to the middle of the room was fun. They grabbed towels out of the opposing team's hands, passed, protected, and fought. The only restriction I placed on the game was no kicking, punching, or getting off hands and knees. The game built shoulder strength and mat motion agility. They learned important skills while conditioning their bodies. As the season progressed, I saw their shoulders straighten up and their strength improve. I got more out of their conditioning by game playing than I would ever have gained by standing in the room and shouting out numbers for push-ups. We also did our share of push-ups, but the players always liked this game better.

When adding games to your coaching, look at the motion in the skill that you need to improve. Then mold it into a game/play situation that builds the physicality of the skill you are seeking in a fun and repetitive way.

Make Better Athletes

It is common for experienced players in basketball, baseball, and especially football to have poor up-and-down hip motion. It is hard work to stay down in your hips. It requires strength and conditioned muscles to maintain a defensive stance similar to what you need to see while defending in baseball and basketball or maintaining a hit position in football or a powerful stance in wrestling.

Every sport uses some variation of the same athletic stance; hips low, shoulders over knees, legs bents, back straight, and head up. Many coaches neglect to improve the core muscle skills required to hold this most essential position. You cannot assume that your athletes are able to hold these critical positions. This lack of physical application to basic stances and the resulting misapplication to important performance skills will be corrected as you improve your coaching skills and remove poor mechanics.

It is common in baseball for a coach to place naturally gifted athletes in key positions in order to win while neglecting the physical development. As a ground ball approaches shortstop, the proper execution of skill is to move your feet until your entire body is in front of the ball and then drop your hips, keep your eyes and head up, get the ball in the glove, get on the balls of your feet, get your feet under you, come up, and make the throw for the out. Yet, how often do we see those mechanics? How often do we teach those mechanics? We see reaching, bending at the waist, and stabbing at the ball a hundred times for every time that we see hips drop and strong positions held. This lack of performance indicates poor mechanics and even poorer coaching.

In football, coaches constantly cry for their linemen to fire out, take big first steps, and stay low, but they spend little time strengthening the hips and core, which is required to perform that motion. It is tough to take three steps forward while keeping your hips low and staying in a good stance position.

With the limited practice time, many coaches spend an inordinate amount of time teaching the complex mental portions of games. In football you can easily consume every available moment learning passes routes, running, and blocking assignments and leave little or no time coaching other portions of the game. It is much too easy to neglect essential physical work. I have seen coaches spend so much time talking about what they want their athletes to do that the practice schedule leaves no time to actually grow and develop the physical skills required to win games. There is too much talking and not enough working.

At the same time, coaches who are too busy for physicality drills readily stand on the sideline and wonder why they cannot win the game. They scream at their kids to do what they have not yet mastered. This double disservice is deepened when the coach blames the kids because they are not "winning," but the coach is the one who has not invested in the equal development between physical skill and intellectual game playing.

Lack of skill improvement is the coach's fault. Every kid can be better at the end of the season than the beginning. But it takes energy to reach all of them. Physicality can only be improved by repetitive drill. Muscle memory improves when the muscles do one thing at least a thousand times.

Couch potatoes will never do up-down motion a thousand times because repetition quickly becomes work until you make it fun. Coaches employ every scheme they can think of to get the talented kids on their team.

We all want great players, but in Little League the majority of the players are not naturally gifted. A quality coach will help every kid improve. I call the process of grabbing the best athletes "cherry picking"—get the most athletic kids from the league talent pool, teach them little or nothing, and take credit for their winning. This conduct leads to several issues:

- What happens to the other kids?
- What about the improvement level of all the athletes?
- What happens to this talent pool in a few years? (The four years between today's twelve-year-olds and tomorrow's high school varsity team goes quickly.)

More times than I can count I have seen neglected kids with tenacity stick with a sport and succeed years later in spite of poor coaching in Little League. Many of those kids were dismissed by their earlier coaches, who were more concerned about their team's ability to win than about developing all their athletes.

Kids change and grow. It is possible for the persistent player to become better than the naturally gifted athletes who were given first team status early in their career.

How Many Kids Are Too Many to Lose from a Sport?

Cherry picking is a tragedy. I am not indicting coaches but rather the process of poor coaching. It is no secret that feeling less valuable to a team can bring about negative and harmful behaviors such as lack of exercise, isolation, despondency, poor choices of friends, drug use, and worse. Not all kids are cut out to be great athletes, but every kid can improve and have a positive experience.

Anyone can cherry pick the best talent. Great coaches inspire, nurture, connect sport to life's lessons, and impact a young person in a positive way. You, as coach, must mentor your athletes using skill, intelligence, technique, and strategy. When the entire process is fun, it becomes powerful for the athlete. Do not be too proud to listen to sound advice, too foolish to comprehend the wisdom of mentors, or too lazy to make necessary efforts to improve physical motion. Physicality is, after all, the foundation of the sporting games that we play.

A Word Concerning Gifted and Natural Athletes

I am not a basketball player. I never was and never will be. I have a few good reasons too. I never played pickup games as a child. We did not have a driveway, and the old hoop that I nailed to the garage wall bent so badly that it was no longer parallel to the ground. I could not dribble, shoot, or pass. No one ever showed me how, and the couple of times that I played in PE, I was "schooled" so soundly that I didn't want to play anymore.

But there is one reason greater than all of my frustration for why I am not a basketball player. It is not in my genes. My best friend in fifth grade was Mike Stewart, a great guy with a love for Superman comics. When we became friends in grade school we had similar body types, or so I thought. That soon changed.

By the time we were in junior high, Mike was twice as tall as I was. By the ninth grade, he was recruited for the varsity basketball team. When we graduated from high school, he stood six feet seven inches, had played on two state championship teams, and was heading to college with a full scholarship. How could I compete with that? Mike's size, so perfect for basketball, was a genetic gift. His commitment to work, combined with good coaching, earned him a college education. But the fact is, Mike made our high school team the moment his parents created him. Those of us who love a sport but lack the genes conducive to that sport have few resources to support our passion. We rely on our personal love for the game, a commitment to work, a desire to improve, and good coaching to go as far as we can. You will coach more "Rudys" than royalty in Little League.

I love the story of LaVell Edwards, the head coach of BYU football, builder of their national championship program, and mentor to players such as Steve Young, Jim McMahon, and Ty Detmer. Coach Edwards understood the power of natural ability. An alumni booster of the Cougars asked what they could do to help build the football program. "Send me bigger and faster boys," replied the coach.

Natural athletes are born standing on third base in terms of their innate capacity for athletic success. The exceptional ones are genetic home runs. The rest of us—the slow, the slender, and the silly—are bunting our way toward first. Natural athleticism, talent, size, weight, and speed are gifts.

Each kid that you coach in Little League will have varying degrees of natural athleticism; some will have none at all. Coaching young athletes requires a constant balance between their natural gifts and how much you can improve their performance and skills. Improving athletic performance requires you to combine fun, physical drills, and character development

In athletics, hard work is the character trait that best serves coaching's purpose. Discipline, tenacity, work ethic, and perseverance are matters of development just like the ability to hit a ball or make a tackle. Coaches who understand that hard work brings success greater than talent alone eventually experience coaching's capacity to affect children's lives and create phenomenal experiences within sports. Coaches who fail to recognize their obligation to develop the complete child shortchange their own coaching experience.

During high school, my greatest talent was hard work. My father told me that if I moved sprinkler pipes on the farm all summer I would be a great wrestler. Do you know what I was? I was a great sprinkler pipe mover and was happy at the start of each school year. I wrestled, ran, played football, and cheered for my friend Mike while he made basketball look easy. Our culture tells our children two big lies: 1) it's easy and 2) you can have it now. Any success I ever gained as an athlete was the result of work more than talent.

Coaching Is a Journey, Never a Destination

The foundation of all sports is kinetic motion, the physical activity required to maintain the body of an athlete through movement as they play the game. The technical accuracy of physical action is improved through repetition. The more physical motion is correctly rehearsed, the better athletes can execute the motion that sports and games are built on. Muscle memory is an interaction between the brain and nervous system. In sport science it is known as proprioception, or the ability to sense the position, location, orientation, and movement of the body and its parts. Proprioceptors are the nerve endings that tell the brain where your arms, hands, legs, feet, fingers, and toes are located. In sport science this is known as a kinesthetic sense of awareness. Here are a few examples:

- A person who types without looking at the keyboard exemplifies proprioceptors at work.
- When muscle memory is finely tuned, your athlete throws to first base without thinking because correct technique is ingrained into the memory of her muscles.
- If your quarterback keeps his eyes up, chest lifted high, and runs on his toes while preparing to pass, he does it consistently and correctly because his muscles remember.
- If your soccer player dribbles consistently and effectively, it is because she has groomed the physical skills until they are second nature.

Coaches who overlook muscle memory fail to improve performance and will never fully prepare their athletes for success. Improving every physical skill required for sport is centered in the process of grooming proprioception through the drills and exercises that your athletes consistently perform. Athletes improve athletic abilities through the process of repeating correct movements and rhythms. The age-old coaching axiom holds true—perfect practice makes perfect. I will add, when the technique of the physical skill is correctly perfected. The opposite is also true. If an athlete practices with poor technique or incorrect movement, he or she builds bad muscle memory and destroys good athletic skills. Little League athletes who are taught bad technique will forever be challenged to overcome those ingrained bad habits. As you coach, ask yourself the following questions:

- Are your athletes improving their physical skills?
- Is their athleticism deteriorating on your watch?

Young athletes face a variety of sports that beg their participation. Due to growing competition within high school ranks, more and more young athletes focus on one sport and train for it nearly year round. The importance of early and correct kinetic training with adequate repetitive drill is paramount. Continued access to proven championship instruction is more necessary today than ever before. You limit their potential when you fail to understand and improve physical skills regardless of the level on which you coach or the amount of their raw talent level. I said it before and it bears repeating: coaching is a journey, never a destination.

Coaches who yell at athletes to constantly perform specific skills are drilling them imperfectly. Baseball coaches yell, "Keep it in front of you!" Football coaches scream, "Stay low!" The fact that they are yelling means that they have not taken the time to groom an athlete's ability to perform, or they do not know how to groom athleticism. If your athletes cannot do a skill correctly once, they will do it correctly only by accident during competition. In order to help athletes improve, you must develop correct athletic technique. It is the primary element of consistent performance. Repeated drills improve physicality. Brilliant coaching causes couch potatoes to work hard enough and stay on task long enough to improve their physical skills. Things go better during games. Your voice lasts longer, and you deliver kids to the next skill level. Only work and using correct technique will improve athleticism. Talking will not.

Five Ways to Avoid Making the BIG Mistake

1. Fun

Make the first practice of the season as much fun as possible. Then, systematically draw similar levels of pure fun and play back into disciplined exercise. You do not have to reach every goal on day one, but you must connect with your athletes. Kids play a sport because it's fun. They stop playing the sport when it stops being fun.

2. Use of Time

Assess every five minutes of your workout for an hour. Have a parent or assistant coach keep track of what you do during each moment. It will probably surprise you how much time you spend talking. If the ratio of you talking to them moving is less than three minutes of activity to one minute of verbalizing, you may well be out of balance.

3. Balance

Use your workout log to balance the time spent during practice talking, drilling on technique, working, and playing. Pay attention to what you are doing and adjust accordingly. If your team is not performing in a competition, you must make more repetitive play a part of your workout. The less experienced or new in the sport your kids are, the more they need designed play time that teaches appropriate skills. If your team is not active enough, then your coaching gets out of balance. As your athletes get older and more competitive and focused in the sport, then you can increase the drills and technique portions of your workout and lower your "play" time. But never turn your workouts into a lecture. A quality varsity team may conduct workouts that are one minute of talk to nine minutes of work. Those are very focused and competitive teams, certainly not beginners or youth. Less talking and more working is always the better plan.

4. Copy the Best

If you must talk, then talk like an Olympic coach. I had an opportunity to work with Kevin Jackson, a national and world champion wrestler, Olympic champion, and Olympic development coach for USA

Wrestling, the youth development organization for the Olympic wrestling program. Coach Jackson taught me an important lesson. I watched him work with athletes at the Olympic Training Center in Colorado Springs and noticed that he was well prepared and stopped only long enough to communicate the correct elements of a technique. When he did speak, his speech was to reinforce, correct, and improve physicality. Coach Jackson would teach a skill and then move his athletes into a workout to repetitively drill the move. As he watched, he would ask for more repetition. Each time he saw the technique performed correctly, he would approve: "Good. That's what I want. Again." Not only were his athletes working with great persistence and effort, but the talk that they heard was continuously correcting and supporting their motion.

Here's an important note: The closer the verbal correction occurs to the moment of its rehearsal, the more effective the communication becomes. Imagine playing against a team and then talking about what went right or wrong a week after the game. That does little to effect change. The outcome of games occurs in split-second moments of athletic motion. In order to change behavior, you must recreate the correct motion that you want. If the correction occurs long after the actual moment of physical execution, it only creates awareness but stops short of changing the physical skills that caused the game failures (for example, missed tackles, dropped balls, bad shots). But if you will integrate your verbalizations into the motion that you design for your athletes as you teach them how to perform the skills of the sport, you will be amazed at the change you will see in your athletes. Coach Kevin Jackson does that, and he is an awesome coach. You can be too. Watch the better coaches in your own league and mimic their good behaviors.

5. *Forget You*

Severely limit any talk that involves you rather than them. When you are talking, your athletes are not improving. Yes, coaching requires oral communication and there are appropriate down times when you build relationships, but we are talking about the quality of our workout time. Never lose sight of the short time that you have with them and the great need that is entrusted to you to move your athletes to a better place physically, mentally, and emotionally. Too much talk creates too little motion for kids. Keep everyone involved. When nine kids stand while one is talked to, what does that say to the kids who are standing? Are they not important? Do they not matter? Avoid this trap. Every kid matters, and moving one forward requires moving everyone forward. Success in the team experience flows to the kids through you as you apply these five simple strategies to help them work more and talk less.

Stop Talking and Keep Them Working Correctly

Here's a quick baseball example of game playing to keep them working while fixing the problem of players not moving their feet or dropping their hips to get in front of the ball. Divide your players into two groups and give them a baseball. Have one player toss the ball on the ground in front of the other player so that he or she has to move their feet and keep their hips under them. Make the other player move their feet, drop their hips, and pick up the ball. Just do that much motion, but make them do it correctly. Make it a game. Reward the most correct performances in a row with food, a drink, or whatever they like. Make it fun and they will get the reps they need to improve their performance. Play is unfettered, and it creates a release of energy and diversion that sustains more energy and greater interest. The number of innovative ways to bring physical drills and consistent work into your practice is limited only by your imagination. I cannot tell you how many coaches refuse to learn this simple lesson. Stop talking and find ways to keep the workouts fun.

3

YOUNG ATHLETES ARE A WORK IN PROGRESS

Teach and Nurture, Don't Judge or Discourage

My family fled Africa to create a new life in America. I could have easily found a group of influencers in high school who were not focused on effort and accomplishment. Not only was I able to compete and succeed in a varsity sport, I met friends who continue to help me make good decisions.

—*Mamadu B., College Student*

Now that you are a Little League coach, what will be your personal philosophy, and how will you incorporate it into the daily process of coaching? Because coaches direct activity toward a specified goal, your success is measured by whether you bring your athletes closer to the goal or push them away from it. The process of coaching centers on teaching. Teaching includes nurturing as opposed to judging or discouraging and must be expressed within the context of improving physical skills. Because your team spends more time working together as a group during your practice sessions than they do engaged in competition as a team, one question you must answer is this: how are you going to coach your kids?

My Beginning

I became a coach by default while finishing my undergraduate degree. I was a substitute teacher in our local school district. Because I could handle teenagers, I was often asked to sub at junior high schools. During one assignment, I learned that the wrestling team had a match that afternoon. I went to the match and quickly noticed the interactions between the coach and the boys. The coach was a good man, a well-intentioned teacher who understood teenage boys but knew little about wrestling. The boys were trying their best to compete in spite of hundreds of disconnects between their ability and the skills of the sport. I had wrestled in high school and college, so I felt that I had insights that might be of some benefit. I offered my help the next day at practice. When I showed up in the workout room, the coach greeted me. He seemed grateful for my offer to help and allowed me to conduct the workout. Then he left, and I never saw him again. That was my introduction to coaching. He returned to the classroom, and I began a twenty-five-year exploration into coaching effectiveness. I did not yet know how to coach. I only knew what time practice started and how to open the practice room door.

The Common Ground of Coaching

A coach is the person charged with instructing players, regardless of age, gender, or ability, in the fundamentals of a particular sport. The coach directs those players during competitions or play between teams or individuals. A coach's success is measured in a number of ways. We dig deeper into what defines success later. The process of coaching means that you guide your young charges while imparting knowledge of the game, its play, and in a greater context life itself. Natural by-products of any sport include exercise, peer interactions, constructive play, and time spent in healthy environments. To make the youth experience anything other than that is counterproductive to your role as coach and your service to young people.

The Purpose of Little League Sports

My granddaughter is three and plays soccer. More accurately, she dresses in a really cute outfit (her description), assembles on a field, and mills about for a period of time before having treats. What is her purpose? To have fun, play with friends, get some exercise, and look good. Does she care if she wins? What do you mean win? She *is* winning, although her method of measurement may be different from yours.

Your Purpose as a Coach

To win at all costs is the old-school way of thinking. The new-school definition of winning is a by-product of effort, technique, intelligence, and skill. I coached a wrestler who was a district champion when he was in the eighth grade. At the time, he was exploring every sport in an effort to test his commitment to his first love, basketball. Now, as he enters high school, he has not only made a personal pledge to play basketball, but he has also made the varsity squad. If my focus was winning, I would have worked to keep him on my team rather than wishing him well on his journey into a sport that competes at the same time as wrestling. Not only am I happy for him, but I know that his time with me helped improve his core body strength and developed his confidence. Do I wish he were still wrestling? Absolutely! Am I willing to guilt him because his departure cost me a great athlete? Never! He is more important than the outcome of his contribution to either program. I wish him well, know that I helped him on his way, and cheer his success.

When winning games is more important than nurturing and teaching, you are out of balance. Your actions will eventually be driven by the need to win rather than to serve the best interest of your athlete. I have seen coaches sacrifice future interests of a child to win a game. I do not believe that is right, and it certainly is not in the best interest of the child. But if your goal is to create the most positive experience possible and leave your athletes in a position to take their skills to the next level, then physicality becomes important, fun, necessary, and your compass for coaching.

Few young people play physically enough to build a storehouse of experience through their own activity. The lack of play as part of daily physical activity creates a society of diminishing levels of physical play. Your role is to encourage physical activity so that athletic capacity moves to greater skill levels. To do less is a disservice to your athlete and Little League sports. It is possible for a young athlete's first experience doing a push-up, repetitive foot work, catching or kicking a ball as part of a team, or other athletic skills to take place under your tutelage. Recognize where they are today and work to move them to a greater capacity tomorrow. In this chapter we discuss four foundational concepts: teach, mentor, assess rather than judge, and inspire as opposed to discourage. During the process of engaging and improving child athletes, discouragement comes easily if your focus loses balance. Balance is measured by doing what is best for the athlete in partnership with improving their performance.

Are you coaching in a competitive league where winning is paramount, or are you in a participation league where the mandate is equal participation and experience for each child? These are important issues.

Youth athletics should be a quality experience rendering an increase in cardiovascular activity, a chance to be with other kids, an opportunity for learning how to work in groups, and a positive experience for as many participants as possible. Winning games is part of these processes, but just a part. Undue influence from competition, other coaches and players, or even yourself can challenge the administration of your program and hinder the success of your coaching. Often when a Little League event is over, the children are happy and looking forward to treats. The coaches are the ones who struggle with how their team played. Always remember balance. Your role as coach is to put integrity into your program and bring improvement to your athletes. Winning will take care of itself. In fact, you will win more if you have a balanced philosophy of growth and improvement.

Balancing Teaching and Mentoring

One of the athletes I coach is both a wrestler and a football player. He is an exceptional wrestler. He is wiry and strong, with great natural skills that support wrestling but not football because he is small. As much as he loves football, he will not play in high school, where the players are huge and fast. He is in the eighth grade and weighs seventy-six pounds. Right now he is eating more peanut butter than I would ever care to consume in the hopes that his metabolism will kick in and he might grow closer to 103 pounds (the smallest weight for high school wrestlers) by next wrestling season.

My problem while coaching him has nothing to do with his play. It is his temper. He has an anger issue and buys into our culture's definition of success as indicated by the two biggest lies of our time: you can have whatever you want easily and you can have it all right now. I tell him he only has one problem—his daddy's rich and his mama's good looking. What I mean by that is that he wants everything to be effortless because easy is all he has ever known. He is such a gifted athlete that he won early and often in the beginning of his Little League wrestling career. Now that he is facing tougher competition, his skill and natural ability are tested. When he meets adversity, his first inclination is to quit and let his frustration overpower his personal commitment for work and improvement. He has never been pushed like he is being pushed now. His skill is natural, giving him much success with little difficulty. But in order to continue in the sport, he must discipline himself and increase his level of work. As he moves from Little League to varsity teams, the refining fire of competition will hold him accountable for what he accomplishes. It is a painful journey that must be guided. Too many children, accustomed to things acquired easily, find greater levels of discipline or effort uncomfortable. Paying the required price in training and effort is new to them. Work can seem overwhelming. If not nurtured through this challenging transition, they fail to realize their potential. Good coaching connects the dots between ability, effort, and achievement. True victory is always on the far side of effort.

A Case in Point

My wrestler did very well at a competition one weekend. He placed second in one style of wrestling and third in another. Two tournaments and two medals certainly made a successful outing. In spite of a great weekend, he was not happy. His need for effortless success created panic. But it is more challenging than that. This kid gets crazy when he is not winning—even if he only thinks that he is not winning. I had to manage this panic another time earlier in the season. A few weeks before, while wrestling for the championships of our school district, my wrestler was competing in a semi-final match. His opponent hit a move and tied the score. All my athlete had to do was score one point, something he was more than capable of doing in the thirty seconds remaining in the match. But in that moment, when the win was not coming easily to him, he started to dread the possible, although not probable, outcome of losing while the final score was still unknown. Rather than stay in the moment and continue to compete, he started to panic. From the sideline I did all I could to keep him focused and execute skills, knowing the points would come. I kept him in the moment by relying on the skills we had drilled in practice. He scored three points, winning the match and eventually the tournament.

Competition Defines Improvement

One of the greatest lessons we can teach our athletes is that life is not easy and success comes only after effort. If coaching is teaching athletic skills, then mentoring is guiding emotional responses through competition. The athlete needs to grow, especially when it is not easy. Discipline and work move present capacities forward. I have been coaching my wrestler for three years and hope he stays with us for four more on the high school team. He is a major part of our success and will have a powerful experience if he stays in the sport. But the lack of control over his anger is a challenge to his ability to improve. Last weekend his panic took over again. Following a loss in his final match, he went crazy even though he placed third in the tournament. He lay on the mat, crying and thrashing his arms and legs, so upset that his club coaches were unable to speak to him. Here is the dilemma I faced. A great young athlete had a problem, and I as his coach needed to solve it. If I could not, he would be stopped in his progression. If I could encourage him and work through this problem, he could be one of the truly great athletes in my program and would gain the valuable benefits that participation in a varsity high school sport could give him.[1]

I could have said, "You lost. What do you want me to say?" He already felt like a loser. But he is not. He is a good young man and a

1 **NOTE:** Do not let the process discourage you. It seems like a lot of effort, but with a little practice it becomes second nature to you, just as heads up and quick feet become second nature to your athletes. Professional, Olympic, and collegiate athletes also have mental lapses in mental capability. It is not just a Little League thing. It is a coaching thing, and it will continue for as long as you coach athletes.

great athlete, but his point of reference tells him that he is a loser due to the outcome of a single match. Destructive self-labels are preposterous conclusions, but many of our children are labeled by themselves and others. His worldview comes from the "winning is everything" mentality. Here's how good coaching bridges this gap. I cannot say, "We'll get him next time," because in his current state of frustration there will be no next time. Saying, "You have to get better," is a small consolation and inadequate motivation. My role as his coach goes beyond his physical ability to an attitudinal arena. Because I have a good relationship with this athlete, I can facilitate what I need to happen. His potential is great enough and he is getting old enough that losing control of his temper has to stop. We had a pretty terse conversation following his meltdown. My direct confrontation was supported by our excellent relationship, but in that moment while bringing him back to my team, I sensed three key elements to affectively changing his attitude and keep him moving forward in the sport.

Keys to Success During a Critical Mentoring Moment (SIG)

- **S**hare a vision by establishing clear boundaries for what is expected.
- **I**ncrease your expression of appreciation for his or her participation on the team.
- **G**ain commitment for a future level of effort.

Young athletes, especially young men, require and respond to boundaries. They need to know where the edges lie in the work that is necessary for success and in the manner of effort that you require as coach. During this teaching moment, I had to make my athlete know that this behavior was unacceptable. I needed to set that hook with very stern (but not mean), uncompromising authority.

As I sat with my athlete, I realized that we were beginning a pivotal teaching moment. Teaching moments have a structure to them that facilitate positive outcomes. They occur quickly and often, so you must be prepared to handle them. After he cooled off, I let him know how important he is as a person and as an athlete. I then reinforced the situation so that he knew that he had gone too far. He had stepped over the edge of acceptable behaviors. His anger was not helping his improvement or moving him toward his own goals. We were having a conversation about a boundary that he cannot keep crossing, or else he will stop his own athletic development.

Using the Three Keys

S—Share: I told him that he is going to do great things. I shared our team vision, something that we have been cultivating for three years, and let him know that we cannot reach our goals without him. He is an integral part of our program.

I—Increase Appreciation: I then increased my appreciation for him by articulating an experience where he showed exceptional performance. I talked about this anger and how it is negatively impacting his ability to grow and improve. I also told him that losing games or competition is part of a sport. If he looked around, he would see that even though many athletes are losing matches—about half to be exact—he is the only one throwing a tantrum. I also suggested that he watch *The Scout,* a great movie starring Albert Brooks and Brendan Fraser about a baseball player who ultimately discovers that half the players win and the other half lose during every game. Only when Fraser's character comes to terms with that simple reality of playing games is he able to free his claim to his unique magnificence.

G—Gain Commitment: I finished our conversation by asking for and getting a commitment that he change this behavior, stay the course, commit to a more focused effort in the one place where he has total control of the outcome (the practice room), and remain a part of our team.

Coaching is a constantly evolving relationship between you and your athletes. Notice there is no room for anger, threats of retribution, or personal attacks. If you need to get your own emotions under control before you have this conversation, do it and then talk to the child in your care. The above keys can guide every conversation. The ABCs of Nurture will also direct your course toward building and maintaining relationships.

The ABCs of Nurture

A—Always be involved.
B —Balance the conversation.
C—Correct where and when you see a problem.

The ABCs of Nurture is a coaching philosophy to help you teach and mentor. You teach physicality, you ask for a commitment from your athlete for their best effort, and you always respect the inner child—who they are and the potential of who they will become. *Nurture* means to continually improve your relationship with each athlete in such a way as to positively reaffirm your concern for their success and growth. The old-school mentality of barking, shouting, and criticizing does not work. If you do that, today's young couch potato will shut you off and refuse to respond to anything you say. They can discard your counsel faster than they stop using out-of-date video games. It is difficult to reach quality levels of connection during a single season. But the concepts hold true and will guide your association whether you coach a team for ten years or ten days.

1. Always Be Involved

One of my favorite rewards from coaching is seeing one of my former players and still connecting with the time we spent together. Last weekend I ran into one of my former football players. He was changing jobs and staying with his parents for a few weeks while his new home was prepared. He reminded me of a conversation that we had about expecting more of yourself and getting serious about education, goals, and so on. Little did I know how strongly he had taken that message to heart and how much it had impacted him. He was not one of the great players on our team. His main sport was swimming. But more than ten years later, the things we had talked about while part of that team still had a place in his heart.

When I run into kids in the neighborhood at the store, church, or school, I always address them as members of the team. They always call me Coach, a title I wear with honor. I am always involved each time I connect with them, even if that involvement is nothing more than recognition or assurance.

One of my Little League football players, now in high school, was injured and on crutches most of his sophomore year. Every time I saw him, I was eager to know the status of his injury, progress of his recovery, and prognosis for his future. I was grateful when he saw me at events and we talked. Knowing you have a positive influence is one of the most satisfying moments of involvement with youth athletics.

2. Balance the Conversation

Balance is critical in what you do and say. Create a positive relationship with your athletes so that when you make a critique, they know you are talking about the game and aren't judging their performance. Talk about event outcomes as if they are a third party. You are the assessor, the communicator, the coach. The outcome of a sports competition creates enough discouragement without you adding to it. Coaches must never point out individuals by saying, "Your tackle cost us the game, because you failed to get a hit in the ninth inning we lost, two more free throws and we would've won." Balance your conversation. There are so many variables in a game that it's nearly impossible to pinpoint one single moment that caused you to lose. Use scores and outcomes as your benchmarks. Improve upon those game-changing moments by focusing on personal assessment and then directing that assessment toward the necessary drills to fix the problems. Be productive rather than making personal judgments equated only to outcome. This is not easy to do. Individual plays affect team score. It is difficult to leave them alone, but you must. The players know what happened and will respond more passionately than you ever can. Leave yourself free to maintain positive dialogue within the culture and shared experience of your team, but move forward by assessing those physical moments and fixing them through repetitive drill.

Base your athletes' sense of self and personal well-being on how they are coached, what you think of them, and how they are improving in the sport, not on what happens during a single moment of a game. Kids already put more than enough pressure on themselves when something goes differently than hoped. Even in beginning leagues, when scores are not kept, the kids come up with an assessment to show why someone is better than someone else. After all, we are coaching in America. Everyone wants to win. Kids want to win easily, and parents want to win often. Coaching is not easy. It takes time and yields bounteous rewards when things are kept in perspective and balanced.

The Kids Make Assessments—You Need Not

During a Little League event, we gave gold, silver, and bronze medals to the top three players and a smaller participation medal to every other kid. I heard a young athlete who won a silver medal ask another kid to see his medal for participating and then smirked. "Oh, you got one of the loser medals." So much for protecting frail little egos. But to Grandma and Grandpa, the participation medal was positive and appreciated within the greater context of a child's potential.

Most of the kids you coach are overly protected. They readily transfer any kind of performance criticism into discouragement. Enriching children's experience is always difficult, so stay away from any ineffective or harmful practice of personal discouragement. You must affirm good behaviors and show ways to improve while giving reasons for that improvement. Your strong example of a structured workout, even tempered handling of challenging situations, and most important, a sincere interest in what is best for each child will serve you well. The dialogue between the team, assistants, and parents allows you to manage your team's experience and gives athletes an opportunity to move to better performance and have greater fun.

3. Correct Problems, Whether Physical, Attitudinal, or Effort

Correction is always supported by physical redundancy. For example, if a baseball player misreads a game situation and throws the ball to second base when he or she should have thrown it to third base, then the problem to correct is physical. Simply telling the player, "Throw the ball to second base next time," will rarely change the behavior. More often than not, the next time a similar situation presents itself, the same mistake will be made.

How Do You Fix That?

You fix mistakes through repetitive drill to create muscle memory. Go back to your workout, create a scenario as similar as possible to what happened during the competition, and run it again and again. Involve your entire team, not just the one committing the game error, so that they physically move through the motion of that moment in the appropriate way. As they do it, coach each element within the skill. You cannot say to any athlete at the end of the game, "You know if Johnny would have stepped up and thrown that to third instead of second, something would have happened." Even though that may be true, you cannot know for certain. Several different outcomes could have happened just as easily. We think we can control so much when in fact we can only control ourselves. Singling out a player for losing the game will always have negative results. Every player will make mistakes. Coaches make mistakes too. Mistakes made early in a game do not seem as important as the same mistake committed in the final two minutes. Pointing to the performance of one player as the game-breaker is counterproductive to the overall success of your program.

Look at the Power that A-B-C Gives You

An old-school coach would shout at an offending kid. My method assesses the problem as something to be solved, knowing that the solution comes through precisely directed effort and work rather than diatribe. Balance your conversation so that you and your athletes create partnerships. View together your assessments of the moments of the competition and what to do to correct them. Commit with your athlete to work together to improve technique, skills, and physicality. Then correct the problem using sport-specific drills, technique, and positive video game reviews. Losing is painful and winning euphoric. Manage each. The winning plays, competitive moments, and individual efforts that create victory elevate themselves. Enjoy them just as your kids and parents will.

My investment in Little League is portrayed in the pictures on the next page of my sons and daughters. Together we created great memories. They grew healthy and strong bodies and learned much about themselves, while I watched the entire process. Good children, strong members of society, responsible parents, and good people—for me, that is the purpose of Little League.

adidas
UtahState

4

YOU CANNOT COACH WHAT THEY CANNOT DO

Discovering the Composition of Competition

During active duty, I am the flight surgeon moving wounded warriors from action to hospitals. In Coach Mike's world, intelligence and curiosity were welcomed. I appreciated that his philosophy was more than just winning.
He helped a gangly teenager grow confident. I have a good family now and work as a trauma surgeon in my community when not called up for Air Force duty.

—*Phil G., Trauma Surgeon*

DURING ONE OF MY FAVORITE episodes of *Seinfeld,* Jerry returns to his apartment. He quickly goes to the television and rewinds the VCR tape that recorded that evening's baseball game. The phone rings. Jerry answers and immediately tells the caller that if they know the outcome of the game not to mention it. He wants to watch the game, and knowing the outcome will spoil his evening. He is reserving the joy of a good baseball game watched in the comfortable silence of his apartment.

Of course, Kramer crashes the door and says, "Boy, did those Yankees stink tonight!" Game over.

What is the purpose of watching the game if you already know the outcome? It's fascinating to watch the human body in motion. Sport becomes more than just win/loss records because of the physical skill required to perform the movements pertinent to the game. Sport is more than merely points scored. The physicality of athletes in action is of itself interesting. I recently attended an NCAA Division I track meet. My daughter was the only athlete I knew, but I loved every moment spent watching the competition. Seeing athleticism and physicality at that level is amazing. The eight-hour day flew by.

The ESPN Classic sports channel is also evidence that there is an audience for sports even when outcomes are known. Physicality is compelling to watch regardless of the sport being played. If your only paradigm for enjoyment is winning, then you lose a major part of the sporting experience.

The Powerful Secret of Physicality Assessment

During Little League football practice, I was standing on the sideline with another parent as the boys ran through plays. I heard the coach yell, "Did you see that?" Something happened during a brief moment, but the coach was the only one who saw it. He tried to share what he saw, but simply talking about it was ineffective. In a split second with twenty-two bodies flying together, an important moment took place. It might have been a missed block, or perhaps a hole opened in the line and created a seam for the running back. Would a running back recognize that split-second seam, react to its brief opening, and move into it? Would any athlete recognize that same moment that the coach saw? How do you teach that same moment to the young athletes that you coach? Our coach saw that moment and shouted, "Did you see that?" But he had no idea how to recreate that moment and offer a teaching moment. You can only coach what your athletes can do. They must understand what you want them to do before they can do it. If they cannot do it, you cannot coach it. You must create ways for your athletes to see specific moments as you see them. Great coaching comes from the acquired capacity to see those little moments, realize what they are reflecting in relation to your athlete's ability to perform the game, and then turn those momentary revelations into focused practice. If your athlete cannot perform a specific skill such as recognizing a developing seam in the line for a football running back and then running to it, you cannot coach that skill during a game. You can yell for it to happen, hope that it happens, or curse when it fails to happen. But until you discover the single moments that compose athletic competition, you will struggle in coaching. Too many times we react to what they cannot do, act as if it should be understood when it is not, and then fail to take the time necessary to teach it. The composition of competition is revealed in the little moments when athletes and action collide.

In baseball, if your infielder cannot drop his hips, you cannot coach that skill. No matter how frustrated you get because your infielders let ground balls pass through their legs, you will not change it until you help them develop the ability to drop their hips. I have seen hundreds of Little League baseball coaches yell and plead with the players to perform better. Yet, when those same coaches have a chance to improve physicality during workout, they choose to have batting practice, where one kid gets to work and the others stand around.

If a soccer player cannot dribble and pass, you need to measure the amount of time that you spend during a workout to improve those sport-specific skills. It is critical that you talk less and work more. Your athletes have short attention spans. You get more intensity during your workout if you design drills or games that match the physical skills you want to improve. Play those games and run those drills until adequate redundancy is achieved to improve motor skills.

If a football player cannot make open field tackles, it is because they are not dropping into their hips, keeping their feet active and moving with head up and back straight, and then driving up and through the contact. No amount of telling them to move in correct ways can ever take the place of hundreds of correct repetitive exercises. While you correct their motion, keep breaking it down to even smaller parts, always looking for perfect technique. They must walk before they can run.

These examples go on and on in every sport. Coaching means you develop coordination and muscle strength, and understand the game. You never stop instructing until your athletes rise to better levels of performance. Your role as coach, teacher, and mentor is to bring your athlete from comprehension of a physical skill to a seamless capacity to perform that skill during competition. As athletes mature, they become stronger, bigger, and faster, while the technique of physicality remains the same. Imagine what could happen if every Little League coach developed athletes to their greatest physical potential before they became teenagers. You can see the effect of grooming muscle memory by watching any professional level of baseball. We have an AAA minor league baseball team in our town. As players warm up to throw, you see them carefully keep shoulders high, step, and throw with a high overhead hand. They repeat this motion each time they throw until they are ready to play. The same is true for batting. They go through a very precise routine to get ready to hit, a mechanical action they have groomed for a lifetime. This is done in the attempt to duplicate physical motion and remind muscles to perform correctly for the best possible results during competition.

How to Make Athletes Perform Better

Let me share a technique for improving athletic performance. This learning process is the result of watching a lot of kids make mistakes and searching for a way to help coaches move through a simple process that improves athletic skill.

ACRE—Assessment, Cognition, Redundancy, Execution

The "did you see that" moment described earlier represents the beginning of the recognition process. You must first see something that needs to be fixed during the athletic performance and then commit time during practice to fix it through repetitive drill.

A Little League All-Star coach approached me recently and asked how to teach a simple routine play. He had just lost a semi-final game in the state championships by one run because of three players who made simple errors. He is a good coach and spoke with great encouragement to his team without placing blame on any one player. The team executed well but committed critical errors that ultimately decided the outcome of the game. I rehearsed to him the same process we discuss here.

Step 1. Assessment

One of the missed plays was a simple cover assignment. The second basemen failed to cover the bag when the shortstop made a great stop.

It was one of those hits that everyone, including the second baseman, thought would go through the infield. But when this great Little League shortstop came up with the ball and turned to throw it to second base, no one was standing there. He then had to reposition his feet and throw to first base. The runner was safe. They missed the force on second base. The runner eventually scored, and that one single moment became the difference between winning or losing the game. The first question you must answer is, what is the problem? Then break down the motion involved. In the above example, did the second baseman or the shortstop commit the error?

In football, a blocking back overrunning his assignment may not be dropping down into his hips. He is keeping his legs extended as he runs, and when he needs to make a quick change of direction, he is not in a stance or hit-position; his feet are not under him. He cannot drive off the appropriate leg. To assess what happened, you disassemble the problem into its individual components of physical motion that surrounds or contributes to the problem you need to fix. You may watch video footage to see it better. Slow-motion replay is a wonderful thing. I remember a ten-year-old football player who was the fastest kid on the field in a straight run, but he was easy to tackle. His coaches could not understand why. I started watching his feet and noticed that when he cut to change direction, he pushed off the wrong foot. If he wanted to cut to his right, rather than push off his left foot, he pushed off the right. It was awkward. The problem was changing direction; the assessment showed a biomechanical problem. He had developed an ability, probably on the playground, to change direction without planting the foot opposite from the direction he wanted to go. Because he had great natural ability, he was moving away from and past other kids on the playground but doing it with poor mechanical technique. On the playground it was no big deal, but eluding tacklers in a game of physical contact required better technique. His physical ability to change was not going to take place without repetitive drill using correct physicality to change incorrect biomechanics.

Step 2. Cognition or Understanding

When my baseball coach friend understood the moment during the championship game that needed improvement, his next step was to make sure his athletes understood it as well. Because merely talking about the problem cannot affect biomechanical change, he needed practice time to fix the problem. Cognition means that both you and your athletes understand the problem, what you are trying to correct, and how you are going to improve it. This is a time when you must talk. You have to effectively communicate. The practice method for fixing this moment for the above mentioned second baseman would be to gather all athletes at second base. Then recreate the moment by actually hitting the ball to the shortstop while walking the second baseman to the cover position and making the throw until everyone understands what took place during the game and how they misplayed the situation. I would then line up every kid, allowing each to take a turn at each of these critical positions. You repeat the correct scenario again and again by letting all of your team members have a chance to perform the play and make the appropriate skills. It also gives all of your kids a chance to be part of the solution as everyone works to rehearse the correct play. In the moment of the physical activity, you have to be smarter than your kids. When you ask them if they understand the skill, they always say yes. In reality, they usually have no idea what you are asking. Communicate. I'll discuss effective communication in more detail later. Right now make sure that they understand by repeating the correct skills and letting everyone participate.

Step 3. Redundancy

Getting the Little League player to automatically move to second base without thinking will require a number of redundant executions of the desired skill. In Idaho we call it work. I know that the word *work* is not politically correct since young couch potatoes are rarely required to actually do any work, but work creates reality out of potential. Work changes bad practice into correct performance. While coaching athletes, you will always see their improvement on the other side of the effort. You are dealing with muscle memory, and changing or establishing the memory of a muscle always takes repetitive effort.

I have a garbage can that sits under my desk on the right side of my chair. When I throw a piece of paper away, my muscles remember that the garbage can is on the right. Try this. Move your garbage can, phone, computer mouse, or any other thing that you repeatedly reach for during the day to a new location. Then every time you move to use that item, your muscles will reach for the old location before your mind remembers there is a new one. Leave it there for a month, and for the next thirty days you will remember this exercise every time you reach for that item because you will always first reach for the item in its old place. That is the strength of muscle memory. It is powerful. Use it to help you be a better coach. If you want to be a great Little League coach, put your athletes through exercises enough times to let the muscles remember so that the following will happen:

- When you need to throw to third, it will be there.
- When you need to see heads up as your athletes lower hips to stop a ground ball, it will happen.
- When you need a game-saving tackle, your kid will drop hips, look at the chest and not the eyes, and drive through the tackle while keeping head up.

Muscles will remember longer and more effectively than the mind of a young couch potato. Athletic performance follows as you take the time to develop physicality. Create a drill. Run your team through the drill until the muscles remember. Intellectual agreement alone will never facilitate physical change. Kids intellectually remember what you want them to do during athletic competition over time. Their muscles remember more quickly and hold that memory longer than their brains do. Never cheat the law of the harvest. Put the effort in. Reap the reward. Applaud great effort with food, swimming, praise, or movie parties. If your kids have fun while working, their couch potato bodies will remember the skills they practiced.

The Power of Muscle Memory

While watching the NCAA Women's Softball World Series, I noticed a pitcher with an interesting habit. Following every pitch, she caught the catcher's throw, walked back to the mound, and signaled the number of outs to her fielders. I am certain that she did not realize she was doing that. In fact, she probably could not stop doing it if she wanted to because it was a muscle memory. It would be an interesting story to know how she came to redundantly set that consistent physical routine, and an even more interesting one would be if you asked her to not do it during the next game. I would wager that her muscle memory would not allow her to stop raising that signal of outs earned without constant reminders from her coach or teammates.

Step 4. Execution

Execution means that during a particular situation, your athlete performs the correct motion or skill that best suits that situation and performs it with the correct technique. In short, execution means doing without thinking and doing it correctly. When skill is correctly rehearsed, drilled, and performed enough times for the muscles to remember, the required motion becomes second nature and the right execution during the game almost assured. Granted, some young athletes with great natural skills do many things well. Your job is to improve everyone's performance and skill levels. You are constantly developing the physicality of your athletes in combination with their mentality and experience with the game. The physical game drives the mental one, the "chess match."

In addition to conditioning a body to physically play, you must train the mind to intellectually do what is best in any given moment. Anyone who has ever coached T-ball knows what I refer to here. When you stand on first base with a five year-old, say run home, and watch her little legs carry her to the place where she eats and sleeps, you will understand.

A Few Ideas for Using the ACRE Model

How do you teach baseball players to hit the cut off man? Suppose that you already have determined the problem and taught what needs to be corrected, and now you want to redundantly reinforce the technique. Make it fun. Use a punch dummy, one of those blow-up dolls that has a heavy weighted bottom. When you punch the dummy, it rolls over and then stands back up. Put one of those in the field where the cutoff man should be, and then let your athletes throw the ball at the dummy. Your kids will have a great time because they will spot the throw, and every hit topples the dummy over, which stands it back up again. Be sure to run every athlete around the bases while you drill. Involve everyone. Change positions. Let them have fun, and they will improve. While they are knocking the stuffing out of that bag (which they will do with great enthusiasm), stand back and coach other physical elements—where their hips and eyes are, if the arm goes over the top, if they land on the correct foot when completing the throw, if the runners are taking three quick steeps to start their sprint. Add catching a ground ball or a fly ball to the drill or any other variation. Most important, you will have employed the ACRE Model: recognize the problem, isolate the skill, teach it, replicate a game situation, and then let your athletes—all of them—run through the drill.

How do you teach baseball players to slide? Get out the hose, wet the ground, and let your athletes get dirty sliding into base. You stand on the side and correct the position as they each execute the skill. Once again, break it down, isolate the moment that you want to teach, and let everyone have fun.

How do you teach stance to wrestlers? Put two athletes on one side of a rolled up mat and instruct them to drop into a staggered stance with their hands extended forward and pressing on the mat. They must keep shoulders over knees as they push the mat. First I have them roll the mat while maintaining good stance, and then I give them resistance by standing on the other side and pushing back. Eventually I put two wrestlers on the other side and let them have a push battle to move the mat. The technical coaching is to keep them in their hips, using back, legs, and arms to push or resist. They will have a tendency to lean and push with their body in a straight line rather than in a stance position.

Little Leaguers Come in All Sizes

The two pictures on the next page are of the same athletes. The difference is about five years of time, growth, and exercise.

We can never overlook the fact that a child is a work in progress. If we do not understand, support, and respect the honor we have to coach children, then we are in danger of doing more damage than good. The measurement of great coaching is in the child rather than the game. As we wisely invest in our children, the opportunity to replenish our future takes place one practice at a time. As we protect the play of our children, we generate strength in our own lives and a possibility of power in theirs.

UTAH

5

HEY, COACH! WE DID THAT ALREADY!

Six Simple Secrets that Teach Work Ethic

> I was out of control and very quick to anger when I entered high school. I was aggressive and not afraid to fight until Coach Mike got me focused. Senior year I was an undefeated state champion because he was my coach and taught more than winning. My love of competition, lack of fear, and ability to do difficult things helped me become a doctor.
>
> —*Marshall B., Doctor of Sports Medicine*

Today's young athlete possesses a need for instant gratification and a lack of work ethic that will make you crazy until you learn six simple secrets. I cannot tell you the number of times that a simple direction to warm up creates opposition. A coach's call for minimal effort is often met with resistance and whining. "I'm too tired." "We did that already." "Again?" Yet, warm-up is part of the game for a number of very good reasons: it gets the mind away from preceding activities, it begins moving the muscles in systematic ways geared to your specific sport, and it literally warms the muscles by increasing heart rate, blood flow, and breathing. When you neglect the warm-up period, you lose a valuable moment to protect your athletes and reinforce the skills that they use to generate success in competition. Some coaches think that kids are lazy, but I think that most do not know how to work. They have yet to understand the importance of physical engagement. Each part of practice is important and cannot be neglected. As Little League coaches, we often move our kids into athletic activity too quickly. Yes, we are pressed for time. Yes, it requires discipline to get a team of young people moving in a singular direction. But when we neglect proper warm-up, we are damaging our athletes in two ways. It is physically dangerous to begin athletic activity without proper warm-up and stretching, and you hinder the overall success of your team by not resetting the core physical motions of your game or sport. Both require work.

I have often heard coaches brag about the great game they just played and how the kids were in a zone. Being in a zone is easier to do with proper warm-up and strengthened by repetition of the skills required for the game; skills that you are teaching during workout and practice. Why would you not use your warm-up time to reset your workout and physicality drills right before the game? Good coaching uses every opportunity to improve and nurture. Great coaching raises the level of effort from every member of your team.

Physical Danger of Bad Work Ethic

I was watching my thirteen-year-old son play a baseball game. I had watched the team the week before when a boy they call Blue pitched. He was a big kid and threw the ball hard. As I watched him during the previous game, I noticed how much power he had in his shoulders. Unfortunately, he failed to support that action with anything from his feet to his waist. He just reared back and threw. His feet landed differently on every throw. His control was all over the place. During those erratic times when he actually put the ball down the middle, he had a solid pitch. Unfortunately, he was doing it only with arm strength. He was entering his adolescent growth spurt with rapidly developing muscles that needed correct developmental technique and exercise. Without proper mechanics, he was in danger. He was big enough and threw hard enough to injure his arm. I asked Blue if he was going to pitch that day.

"No, I can't."

"Why not?"

"The doctor said I strained my arm and I can't pitch for two weeks."

"What are you doing to help it?" I asked.

"I'm taking Ibuprofen."

"I mean, what exercises are you doing?"

"I'm taking Ibuprofen."

Once again, I was talking to a couch potato. The danger to Blue was not that he was injured—muscle strains are common in all sport—but that he was not properly rehabilitating the injury and taking the proper course of action to prevent further injury. Yes, he needed rest, but he also needed a recuperative process that included the biomechanics of stretching and movement to help heal the injury and prevent it from happening again. Blue's attitude of drugs as a solution was not his fault. His present dilemma—an injury caused by overuse, a lack of training, and not enough supportive physical conditioning—happened in a litigious culture where doctors often advise a course of least liability to themselves; parents assume that coaches create all the exercise their children need to be safe and improve their physical performance; and young athletes have yet to learn, like every successful athlete, coach, and parent, that effort, trial, error, failure, and persistence are required for improvement. The doctor said not to do something, so Blue did not. Please understand that I am not a doctor and I am not giving you medical advice. I am simply pointing out that we are quick to let medication be an excuse for helping the body heal, repair, and restore its own athletic ability. You should certainly seek medical counsel. Be wise in training, recovery, and healing.

The General Danger

Teams that fail to work consistently through warm-up, practice, and competition lose an opportunity to successfully prepare for competition today and position themselves for higher competitive levels tomorrow. Blue's Little League team would arrive at the field, drop their bags, and start tossing baseballs. Their warm-up included throwing a few times, sometimes taking a limited infield, and stepping to bat. They did no running, leg warm-ups, stretching, muscle memory for arms or torso, and of course, no sport-specific drills to reinforce correct mechanics for swinging, hitting, running, or throwing the ball. When I suggested a regimen to their coach, he said it was not necessary and they didn't have time. Playing a game without a proper warm-up is like jumping out of bed from a deep sleep and rushing to shut off a burst water pipe. You get it done because you have to, but you do it without preparation or joy.

Six Secrets to Establishing Work Ethic

1. Stay Ahead of Their Attention Gaps

Little league wrestling teams are a kick. They are fun because little kids, especially boys, are so hungry for rough and tumble play that they just go crazy. Kids who have never been in a wrestling room take off their shoes and run wildly across the matted floor so they can bounce off the padded walls. I watched a four-year-old boy run until he met a line drawn on the floor. Then he ran along the line. Wrestling rooms have ten-foot circles drawn on the mat. This little guy started following the line, which of course took him round and round. The faster he ran, the bigger his smile. He eventually fell down, dizzy and out of breath from the exertion and his confused equilibrium. The mat was a soft landing, and there he sat laughing. Parents also like the way little people react to wrestling rooms. More than once I have seen a parent's big smile as her young child ran as fast as their little legs could carry them across the mat. The child's smile was even better.

The foundational truth that I call the "Six Secrets for Establishing Work Ethic Among Young Athletes" began with these little kids. Wrestling is a challenging sport to coach because there is so much technique involved. Talking to preschoolers is very different than talking to high school varsity athletes, yet the physical motion they must master is the same. I learned what real attention deficit is while attempting to articulate the complicated physical motion of wrestling to little kids. It made me crazy trying to communicate with them. This failure to communicate ultimately opened my thinking to a new paradigm. Consider the following coaching points for the motion that occurs during a double leg takedown, the most basic movement in high school wrestling:

- You begin in a strong attack position, one hand forward and the other hand down in a blocking position.
- Change your level, take a penetrating step forward, hands lock behind the opponent's knee, trail leg comes to a strong position, head up, back straight, hips under.
- Lift and drive into the opponent at a 45-degree angle and follow your opponent to the mat.

Once on the mat, another skill set is used in order to continue to the pin. That set of instruction sounds complicated, and it is, but when executed in competition it is a single motion that happens in the blink of an eye. And each of those technical components is included in the motion when the skill is done correctly. Try to teach something as complicated as that to forty kids from five to twelve years old. I struggled with that in every workout. I spent more time trying to engage my young athletes in the conversation than they did in learning how to wrestle. The hyper kids would run around. The insecure little people would look at me with big eyes and sheepishly try but had no clue. The disengaged kids wandered away, and the heavy TV watchers were hurting others with WWF (World Wrestling Federation) moves. I felt like someone had dropped a bucket of rabbits and turtles at my feet. Making them move in one direction was impossible. Because the failed effort showed me that I could not change them, I changed myself and started coaching in a new way. I learned to do the following:

- Anticipate and accept their lack of attention rather than being discouraged by it.
- Use their lack of attention to point my way to encourage appropriate physical action.

When my Little League wrestlers want to run, I let them. But I direct that running through an obstacle course over and around mats. I put the entire group through the course and keep them moving. I include a variety of stations on the course and design different stations to match the physical skills that I want them to learn such as jumping, level changing their hips, somersaults, push-ups, cartwheels, and every other skill relative to the sport. Stay with things that they enjoy. Let the kids maintain action for as long as they like it. Too often coaches leave something that is working to go to something else simply because the he wants to. If you are doing drills and the kids are having a great time, stay with it. When a good vibe is happening, especially with younger athletes, let it ride. The key is keeping them on task and practicing skills that develop athleticism. As they work (and they will work if they love the exercise), think ahead to your next coaching moment and move your athletes to it when their interest in the current exercise wanes.

2. *Devise Games to Teach and Create Fun*

I have already given you a number of examples for this key. There is no limit to what you can do with the game playing element of coaching. As you devise games, remember an important component: start where you want to finish. Steven Covey would say to begin with the end in mind. Look at the performance in a game, competition, or workout and decide where your team's weaknesses are. Start there. If your baseball players are not completing throws to bases, then devise a game that lets them throw the ball a little farther than the distance you want them to throw. Isolate the motion so everyone has the opportunity to do it many times. Every sport has specific exercises. Watch other teams as they prepare for competition and see what they are doing. Become a student of other coaches and then revise ideas that will help you find formats that fit your needs while holding your athletes' interest. I have personally learned much from watching other teams prepare. I am not afraid to use anything that I see on a practice field that is valuable and might help my program. Become an innovator and a duplicator of the principles of this book. Constantly look for and create games that teach what you need your athletes to know and do.

3. *Read Your Athletes*

I sat on the sidewalk during an Independence Day parade. The junior high school cheerleaders were walking past following the end of the parade. It was a hot day, and one girl was flushed and sweating. I asked if she was okay. She said that she was, but if she had been playing soccer or softball, I would have made certain that she had enough water and insisted that she get out of the sun. Pay attention to athletes. Watch how they react to work, hits, cold, or heat. Notice if your kids limp or wince. Look at their eyes for concussions, cheeks for flush, sweat for hydration levels, rate of pulse for exertion, cuts and scratches for skin care. Take first aid training from the Red Cross. Many school districts and community colleges offer basic courses that will be worth your time. Read everything you can about coaching safety and exposure to heat, cold, wind, lightning, and other dangers. Asking a child how she feels delivers an incomplete picture. Do not accept that what they say is true and accurate. When they cry, ask them what happened. When they limp, ask them why. Always question, listen, and express interest in what they say and what happened to them.

Examples of Reading Your Athletes

A twelve-year-old football player goes down hard and comes off the field, favoring his arm. Meet him on the sideline. Isolate the arm. Hold it secure without twisting or moving. Look in his eyes. Ask him how his arm feels. He will say that it's okay. Do not believe him. Take his hand in a grip. Tell him to squeeze. A strong hand clasp is good. A weak one or a wincing pain indicates a deeper injury and requires greater caution.

I am not a doctor nor should your observation take the place of one, but you are the first contact. Do not move any part of their body or anything else until you talk to your athlete, recognize their level of response, and discover what happened. Seek emergency medical help when appropriate.

Another example is a thirteen-year-old baseball player who dives back into first base and breaks his arm. He feels a pop and cries out. The opposing player looks up, worried. He does not know what happened, but he knows something is wrong. Be the first to the field. Calm your player. Tell him everything is going to be all right. Look at the arm. Initiate appropriate first aid.

These two injuries happened when I was coaching. Both arms were broken. Other than obvious safety, the value of reading kids is that you build trust and confidence. I hope you never deal with a broken bone, but minor injuries are common. Sprains happen, yet they are unknown to most of the beginning athletes who you will coach. Response to injury varies with age, but a little pain is a lot of pain to someone who has never known any pain. As your athlete sees your concerns for their well-being, they will trust you. Knowing that you have their best interest at heart, they will perform for you. My athletes know that I will never jeopardize their safety by putting them into the game when they are injured. Generating an ever increasing effort from your team is a consequence of trust and commitment between player and coach. You are the adult. You set the example and the tone of the relationship.

4. Work Them Hard, Let Them Rest

Tyler Pearson was a heavyweight on my wrestling team. His nickname was Lumpy. Like most heavyweight high school wrestlers, he was a character; funny, well-liked, and good company. I named a stretching move after him. You do it by lying flat on your back. Whenever my teams have been working hard and they need a rest or I need to talk with them, I simply say, "Lumpy Pearson Memorial Stretch." Flat on their backs they go. They stretch as they relax and listen. They love it. I tell them that Lumpy Pearson was a former athlete in our program and this was his best move. But this isn't true. He was a very good wrestler and a great strength to our team, but I say it anyway and it becomes a favorite exercise and story for all of my teams. The value in the move is that sometimes kids are tired and they need a rest. Other times I need to talk with them, and this move facilitates a quiet audience. It helps establish work ethic because they know that when they are tired I will let them rest. No matter how difficult the work, they know that there is always an end and they will survive.

5. Create Moments of Measured Excellence (Acceptable Efforts)

While working with your team, you encounter moments when you need certain levels of performance. It might be in effort, unified motion, or quality drill. Regardless, using this simple technique helps improve performance and builds work ethic. While coaching football, I watched a coach yell at his team because he did not like the way they were working out. They ran a play. He yelled. Nothing got better. His coaching was falling on deaf ears. It appeared to me that the kids were tired and had little focus on the moment. They were certainly not accomplishing anything. During a water break, I took the coach aside and asked if I might help. My son was on this team, and I was the trainer. The coach usually refused counsel (he was a should-a-been coach). I was pleasantly surprised when he told me to go ahead. Obviously, his frustration level was greater than I thought. I started by asking what he expected. He said, "I want to run through each play in our slot back offense. I want the backs and ends to run the routes, linemen to fire out, stay low, and move the ball forward. Show some hustle and effort."

When the boys returned to the field, I told them I wanted to try something new. I repeated the coaching points. I then told them that as soon as they executed each of the plays to the best of their ability, we could get past this and move to the next part of practice. We ran a play with not much change. I felt that our problem was one of measurement. The boys had no idea what was expected or when the work ended. They were shutting down. I added measurement and gave them an exit strategy to the coaching exercise. I told them that each play had a quality value from one to ten. I asked for a five. We ran a play. I told them it was a three and to give me a seven. They worked harder. The feedback was now immediate. I called that play a seven and asked if they could do an eight. They tried harder and ran the play better. I gave them the eight. Now they knew what was expected and began focusing on the work. I explained that eight, nine, and ten were acceptable levels of work and performance. I said, "As soon as you give me ten acceptable plays, we will move on." For the next fifteen minutes they worked as a team. I called out "acceptable" when the play hit its coaching points. Coach was excited because he saw effort and could point out success. The assistant coaches began fine tuning moments and positions within each play as well. It was very productive. We moved on, and I learned a great lesson. I immediately had a point of measurement that they understood. I call this the acceptable model. The boys had a clearly defined objective. Our coaches were giving immediate feedback that reassured the players of their skill and effort, and poor performance was instantly addressed and corrected. I worked with these boys many times throughout the next couple of years. Their last year together, they were 12–1 and league champions. We used the acceptable model to ask for greater effort on fourth and long, in goal line stands, during workouts, and of course during Lumpy Pearson Memorial Stretches. I still constantly use this technique. Promising a game or other reward at the end of the drill creates incentive as well.

6. Consistently Reward and Reinforce During Workout

In chapter 2, I mentioned what I learned from Kevin Jackson, the national development coach for freestyle wrestling in America. He constantly affirms his athletes' performance. While his athletes work, he says things such as "Good, that's what I want. Excellent. Give me one more of those." I learned from the best. Now, while working with my athletes, I look for opportunities to personally acknowledge the good things that I see. I say "Nice job, Jenson," or "That's a good effort, Jones." More than once I have seen a smile come over an athlete's face when he or she realized that I not only saw but recognized their work.

Several things happen when you affirm the effort of your athletes:

- The closer that feedback occurs to the moment when athletic skills are performed, whether correct or incorrect, the more effective that feedback becomes.
- They know you are watching what they do and that you appreciate their effort. Acknowledging their effort, presence, desire, and work is meaningful.
- Quality, sincere, and positive feedback is important whether correcting poor work or praising good efforts.
- Effective rewards can be simple, but it never hurts to provide a drink or treat at the end of practice.

A Final Comment on Warm-Up and Work Ethic

Always warm up. That sounds like a simple solution, but with creativity and a few important constructs you can do it. You must warm up to avoid injury, set physicality, and get your athletes out of their day and into the game.

While coaching a junior high school wrestling team, I worked on this concept of innovation for warm-up. My goals were to get the kids warm, break the monotony of beginning a workout, and coach them into the joy of work. Sometimes I tricked them into the joys of work, but they were having so much fun that they called it something else—play.

I had been away from the junior high ranks for several years. I was coaching at the high school varsity level and returned to junior high when my youngest sons moved through the program. I had two goals: spend time with my own boys and test what I was learning. My athletic director, a good friend with whom I had coached nearly ten years earlier, told me that Friday practices were best attended when held before school. I am not much of a morning person and thought that getting kids awake and to school nearly two hours early would be a problem. Surprisingly, it wasn't. They attended regularly, and many of our morning workouts were the most productive of the week. As the season progressed, the level of excitement about working out diminished. Wrestling is a tough sport that requires consistent hard work. On these early mornings, slower starts were affecting our ability to get going. Wrestling is too demanding to ever neglect warm-up. My team needed to wake up. I needed to constantly condition them to physically get through a competitive match. I was constantly seeking ways to nurture technique at the same time. One morning, as I watched them stumble in half asleep, I noticed a box of Frisbees in the coach's office. The gym, which was usually occupied by the girls' volleyball team, was empty. I started throwing Frisbees to my wrestlers. Pretty soon they were tossing them at each other. As soon as I had about half as many Frisbees as athletes, I instructed them to keep the Frisbees in the air. I started my stop watch. It was simply amazing to see them come alive as they played. The action of throwing loosened their shoulders. The motion of running elevated their breathing and heart rates. They smiled as they took aim at each other across the gym floor. Ten minutes later, I called time and took them into the wrestling room for agilities and stretching. The result of this simple warm-up method was fantastic. They were loose and laughing. It proved to be a great way to start a workout rather than the typical morning jogging around the wrestling room.

Get creative with your warm-up process. As often as you can, incorporate some aspect of the game as well such as footwork, foot speed, short sprints, standing jumps and other plyometric exercises, and so on. Here are some warm-up suggestions for baseball and football players:

Baseball Players

Have your players drop their mitts on the ground, pick up a ball, and choose a partner. Then start a jog around the field. As they run, they toss the ball back and forth. This will improve hand-eye coordination. The absence of a glove will sharpen their skills. As they run past you, point out areas of improvement such as catching with both hands, following the ball to their hands, keeping their eyes on the ball, staying on the balls of their feet, and catching the ball in front of their bodies. Allow them to talk but only while working. They will jog along talking, laughing, and challenging themselves. You need not worry about it being fun. They will devise games. They will toss the ball out of reach, toss from behind their back, toss it in the air, and more. You might challenge them to count the number of catches.

Here's another variation. Put several of your young couch potatoes in a line with a ball. Then have them start to jog and follow the fence line. The person in front has the ball and tosses it into the air as high as possible. The last person in the line sprints to the ball, catches it on the fly, and then sprints to the head of the line and resumes the jog. He or she then tosses the ball for the last person in the line. You can do this with or without gloves, but I like it without gloves because hand-eye coordination gets sharper. You make the decisions based on your team's athletic levels.

Football Players

A great warm-up for football is to let everyone get a touch on the ball. Linemen love this because every Little League football player is a quarterback if the coach would just realize it. Set your athletes at three different starting points: a quarterback, a receiver, and a defender. Set a short route pattern for the receiver. Have each athlete run the same route. Let the defender defend and even intercept if possible. Use this as kids arrive for practice. Start with the first three and add them to each group as players arrive. Do not run full speed; it's just a warm-up. Run them all through the stations. Everyone gets to throw a pass, run for a pass, or defend a pass. When they are breathing hard, add a distance run before stretching. Never stretch without warming the muscles first.

Get involved, volunteer, ask questions, and be a solution. Nothing is more dangerous than assuming that the neighborhood Little League program has its act together. Your first impression of the kind-hearted person willing to coach is no indication that they have the skill, desire, or vision to leave your child better at the end of the season than at the beginning.

On the next page is a picture of me with some of the athletes I have coached. I coached the athlete on the left for six years. He was an All-Stater in three sports. His mother is the woman on the far right. The next athlete is one I coached in high school; he is now our head wrestling coach. I'm in the center, the original gangster. Next to me is my son. We

were in Virginia at a national competition. As I look at this picture now, I remember personal development, good friends, strong young men, a better future for each athlete and our program, and good food in Virginia Beach.

6

FEEDBACK IS AN ART FORM

Instantly Improve Your Communication

> I was the skinny kid that no one believed in and the last chosen for games, until I walked into Coach Mike's wrestling room. He believed in me and showed me that I was much more than anything I had done to that point. My senior year I was a team captain. I learned how to finish, and I reached my personal goal. Today I am a US Army Ranger.
>
> —*Chris G., US Army Ranger*

Two high school football teams were playing a game on a sunny and brisk fall day. I was watching from the sideline and began a conversation with a fellow Little League coach. He was a good man who volunteered a lot of time to our league, but he was a lousy communicator. As we watched our sons and other boys we have coached, he began commenting on their play. I tried to add to the discussion, but he acted as if I had nothing to say. I was not surprised because I knew him. Shared meaning was not something that he easily created. In his way of thinking, he knew all there was to know. Why should he listen to me? I had lost any hope of changing his skill set a long time ago and did what I always do when I am in the presence of unknowing: I stopped talking. Yet, as I stood there listening to him, the one-sidedness of the moment made me wonder. Why is he, like so many other coaches, such a poor communicator?

This experience was common. I had seen him speak the same way with young athletes many times, and I had consistently seen coaches talk at rather than to the athletes in their charge. I am a student of conversation. I teach interview and communication on a college level. I constantly listen to conversations in an effort to understand how dialogue breaks down and what it takes to improve elusive communication skills. Because coaching demands an ability to share understanding with others, communication is an important component of quality coaching. Great coaches are great communicators, yet here I was standing next to an active youth coach, one of the better ones I might add, who was poorly equipped to connect with the very children he coached. The reason he was a less than effective coach was not due to the amount of time spent with athletes or his dedication to the league. He had served as coach, officer, dad, and more. He was limited in his ability to coach because he listened poorly, inefficiently responded to his coaching staff and athletes, and totally missed the most important part of communication: feedback. He represented an interesting dichotomy; he was a willing helper and hard worker who could not connect his personal thoughts with those of his athletes. His athletes were hurt by this nonexistent flow of dialogue in two ways: they did not know his intentions for them, and he had no idea what their intentions were for him.

What if I could change his skills? Is it possible to make good communicators out of poor ones? The answer is yes, but you have to be willing to try. You can improve your communication ability and actually elevate its use to an art form if you are willing to examine your current manner of communication. The benefit will be immediate and far reaching. As you make communication effective, it empowers your player improvement. You begin to do the following:

- Evaluate rather than criticize.
- Say positive things during critical moments.
- Control what you say during practice and competition.

- Never speak in anger.
- Ensure that players know you care about and believe in them.
- Listen and respond with improvement in mind.

Communication

Turning poor communication into effective expertise begins by understanding the communication process. There are three components: a message, a receiver, and the feedback created because of the message.

1. Message

A message begins with intelligence; a thought, impression, suggestion, wisdom, or a piece of information that you want to move from your intellect to someone else's. In Little League those messages are meant for athletes, assistant coaches, referees, parents, and administrators. Whether you speak or not, you create a message. Your presence creates meaning. What you say and how you say it becomes your skill.

2. Receiver

Someone hears your message and acknowledges or receives it. At this point, they may or may not comprehend your message. The fact that you send a message does not mean that your receiver got it. Think of the message as if it were a stream of water. You open a spigot to send the water (message). There is a block in the hose and the message (water) stops even though you sent it. You have not communicated yet. The challenge of communication is making sure that the message received is the message sent. Talking to yourself does not create communication. Screaming at young athletes who tune you out as intensely as you yell at them is not communication. Speaking to someone, talking at someone, threatening, cajoling, or weeping in the presence of another person is not communication even though the person who sees, hears, and pays little or no attention to you will receive a message. It will, however, hardly ever be the message that you want them to receive. How can you know the message that they did receive?

3. *Feedback*

Feedback happens because you send a message. Suppose you need your team's goalie to meet twenty minutes before practice. You call (the message), your athlete takes the call and listens (receiver), and the goalie is waiting for you when you get to the practice field (feedback).

We understand the concept of feedback because we see it everywhere. A car dealership advertises a great price on a popular car. Several cars are sold as a result of the advertisement. You want a new camera, search the Internet to find the exact features you have in mind, take action, and buy the new camera. A clear description of goods or services is the message. Advertising, word of mouth, and other pieces of information are carried through print, television, the Internet, and other media. These are the senders. Hearing the ad or seeing the commercial establishes the meaning of the message. Feedback is the resulting action. The communication cycle is completed when the goods or services are sold.

I spent seven years as the public information director for a movie company. One of my duties was to oversee the quality of our conversations with customers. We had seven offices and fifteen hundred employees spending more than two million minutes per month conversing with customers. We looked at feedback constantly as a source of information. By monitoring conversations between our agents and customers, we identified the miscues between the messages we were sending and the information that our customers heard. How they reacted told us the efficacy of the message. We had a small space on order forms where customers could write a note to the company (this was pre-Internet days). I started reading those messages and learned wonderful things. I knew which product was most appreciated. I knew what our customers wanted us to do. I learned to appreciate the feedback stage of the communication paradigm for what it taught me about the message that I sent. I could tell more about the effectiveness of our message through feedback than by anything else. Resales and new orders were the premium indicators of what people heard and understood about our company. By listening to feedback, I learned to adjust the message and correct what failed during our communication. Paying attention to feedback provides a similar service for your coaching skills. It is important enough to say it again: The effect of your communication is the result that you achieve. Below are some examples of feedback:

- A ten-year-old signs up for Little League the year after you coach him. The effect of your communication is another season in the sport for this young athlete.
- A twelve year-old quits playing soccer because she is not happy about the previous season's experience on your team. The feedback might indicate that you were not an effective coach.
- Your assistant coach is frustrated. One of your athletes is missing practice. You lose sight of the moment and direct your assistant to tell the kid "to grow up and get serious." The kid never shows again and you lose him for the rest of the season. The effect of this message is not what you want, unless the intent of your message was to force the kid to quit, in which case, you were very effective.

Three Steps to Effective Communication

Effective communication is a victim of popular culture. The athletes on your team are surrounded by distraction and digital entertainment. They know how to play video games, collect music, and text messages, but expertise in communication is not within their skill set. Ask a boy to download team pictures from a digital camera and he will easily do it. Ask a girl to send text messages detailing the next four workouts, and she will easily do it. Knowing that your athletes hear what you say is not nearly as easy as pushing electronic media buttons, but it is still possible.

Popular culture is no friend of effective communication. The kids you coach spend more time connected to electronic media during a holiday weekend than they spend with you over an entire Little League season. When engaged with videos, games, and the computer, kids control the message and images they want to see and stay with those digital elements for as long as they are entertained by them. When couch potatoes tire of the information or entertainment flowing seamlessly before them, they change it immediately and often. As a coach, you are asking that kids use communication skills that they probably do not possess. To be a great coach, you must become an effective communicator. Here are three steps to assist you.

- Listen to them.
- Keep things in perspective.
- Learn from feedback rather than react to it.

In the comedy movie *Dumb and Dumber,* Lloyd (Jim Carrey), and Harry (Jeff Daniels) are soaking in a hot tub and talking about the reasons they are losers at love. Harry speaks of trying to make things right with a past girlfriend. "I called her up and she gave me a lot of crap about me not listening to her enough or something. I don't know. I wasn't really paying attention."

Exactly. Today's kids are inundated by constant noise, clutter, and personal self-interest. Harry's lack of listening costs him a relationship. Improving personal communication skills enables you to build great ones.

Be the First Good Listener on Your Team

As the leader of your team, it is your duty to become the first good listener on your team. The best listener I ever knew was my friend who was a business manager. If I walked into his office to talk with him, he would always stop what he was doing, make eye contact with me, and give me the full measure of his attention while we spoke. Nonverbal displays of disrespect were never apparent during our conversations. He never grew impatient, looked away, took a phone call, or left my intellectual presence while we were speaking with each other. He was an excellent listener because of his focus and attention on the person standing before him.

Do the same with your coaches, athletes, and parents. During a recent conversation with a business client, the quality of our communication was diminished. He kept leaving the moment by looking at his cell phone. He had the ringer on silent, but his reaction to that technology was more important than our conversation. Some may call it multitasking, but I think it was at best a distraction, at worst rude. In either case, poor listening skills negatively affect our ability to communicate.

1. Listen to Them

Improving your ability to communicate requires the skill of listening. Sending messages is easier than listening to them, though both are important. Listening connects interpersonally transmitted messages. Quality listening communicates honor and respect for another person's time; valuing their opinion encourages the growth of positive relationships; building trust demands that you initiate and manage all elements of communication. Listening connects your message with its intended recipient. The following behaviors indicate poor listening skills. If you are doing them, stop. Correcting these actions will move you along your way to artistic communication. You are a poor listener when you do the following:

- Talk more than listen.
- Text message or check incoming phone calls during a conversation.
- Interrupt what is being said.
- Fail to make eye contact with the person in front of you.
- Jump to conclusions before a statement is complete.
- Attempt to solve a problem before hearing complete information.
- Talk over what another person is saying.
- Talk louder than the person you speak with.

2. Keep Things in Perspective

There is a wonderful piece on Steve Martin's first comedy album. The premise is that Leonardo da Vinci, while painting the *Mona Lisa,* simply takes a glob of paint, splats it on his canvas, and says, "How's that?"

The wonderful absurdity of the moment is that something as glorious and worthy of adoration as the *Mona Lisa* could ever be created from a glob of assorted paint colors randomly thrown against a canvas. I think of that moment often.

Every worthy work, especially creating a work of art from a piece of clay called Little League athlete, takes time, diligence, and consistent application of principle. We are too much in a hurry. Our culture moves quickly, so looking for quick-fix solutions is expected, even anticipated. But coaching is an art form, and the athlete before you is your work in progress. There is no need for haste. There is, however, a cultural imperative to push buttons, find quick solutions, and then move on. Developing a child into a responsible adolescent in preparation for maturity requires lessons consistently learned and daily cultivated. We support athletics because physical play creates an efficient classroom for the growth of our children.

Kids Are on a Greater Journey than Sport

Here is a simple fact. Your team will not win every game even though you want them to. As you keep all things that happen to them in perspective, you maintain an environment that invites communication through a strong relationship with your athletes. The finest TV in the world will never communicate with an audience until the set gets turned on. Coaches guide athletes. Show your athletes how to learn from each contest even though they do not win them all. To expect perfection from imperfect Little Leaguers is fools' play, but we play there all the time. Your tenure as a Little League coach must include keeping three things in perspective for your athletes: the importance of each event, the time in which it occurs in their life, and their development—both physical and emotional—within the sport. Measure every day and the events within it against an athlete's lifetime. Do that and they count their days with you as blessings. They also begin listening to you. A twelve-year-old boy with minimal strength and athletic technique will become an entirely different athlete over the next couple of years because of puberty. His strength increases, and his work ability grows. Let the twelve-year-old boy know that his lack of strength will not be a problem forever.

A junior high athlete who is in their first year of a sport can easily grow frustrated when competing against someone with more experience even though they have greater natural ability. Do not let them be frustrated by their short time in the sport. Keep them engaged by clarifying where they are and where they can go. Kids put tremendous pressure on themselves to win. They watch television and see winning constantly. When it does not happen easily for them, they may throw tantrums. Your ability to keep things in perspective nurtures respect for your opinion as you help them understand that one game, one match, one race, or one event does not constitute a career. One event should never define them. Connect them with what is now and what can be, using optimism toward them, kindness about them, and belief in them. Michael Jordan was cut from his junior high basketball team. It is a good thing for him and the sport of basketball that he did not think himself a loser and quit the sport over that single event.

Communication Grows

When the monster defeats the little guy, it is no credit to the monster. When the monster defeats another monster, it is exciting. When the little guy competes with another little guy, it is sport. Your athletes are growing. Your ability to communicate with them is enhanced as you help them see their world in perspective.

We played a football game once when the opposing team suited up a monster. He was the most talented eleven-year-old I had ever seen. He was quick, big, and athletic, and he singlehandedly won the game. We could not catch him, tackle him, or hide from him. Did his presence mean that we were bad? Not at all. By helping our athletes handle the message that he was sending (he was the monster), they knew that his presence said nothing about who they were. Our message to them was good effort and knowing where we would go from there.

Near my home is a wonderful mountain with a trail to the top about two miles long. I have hiked that mountain often with a group of athletes, scouts, or my own sons. I like this trail because you can see the top of the mountain for most of the journey. When you need to rest, even though you are standing on a ridge, you can still look up and see the top. Good coaching is like climbing that mountain. Help your athletes enjoy the journey, understand the continuum that engages them, and realize that failure in competition is only an assessment of their place on a trail to better performance. The only way to truly lose in athletics is to quit working up the trail. Aristotle said, "We are what we repeatedly do. Excellence is, therefore, not an act, but a habit."[1]

Sport has no end, only glorious bookmarks. The 1972 Miami Dolphins were the last unbeaten professional football team, and they were

1 Quoted from coursework, Philosophical and Psychological Foundations of Education, School of Psychology, Division of Behavioral and Social Science, University of Kentucky.

unbeaten for only one season. No professional baseball, basketball, or hockey team goes unbeaten even though their rosters are full of wonderfully talented athletes. Tiger Woods, the greatest golfer of our time, does not win every tournament. Babe Ruth hit 714 home runs while striking out more than 1300 times.

Stop by any Little League baseball field and watch the game. As soon as a batter strikes out, she fights an inclination to throw the bat and curse her fate. A football player drops the ball, then throws his helmet. A missed shot on goal is met with scorn.

As you become a great communicator, you will help your athletes understand that they are on a continuum. The technique that they have today will be greater tomorrow. Muscles get stronger, motor skills improve, and the intellectual capacity to understand what to do and when to do it advance the longer they remain involved in the sport. Establish perspective for your athletes and maintain perspective for yourself. Learn the skills of communication and use them during every practice and competition.

3. *Learn from Feedback Rather than React to It*

Coaches see all kinds of things—good and bad plays, right and wrong executions of skill, lessons remembered, and workouts forgotten. Suppose you are the coach of a ten-year-old baseball player. You watch from your place on the sideline as he steps up to the plate. You spent yesterday's practice working on his swing and are certain that when the pitch approaches he will step toward the ball, turn his hips toward the pitcher, keep the bat in a poised position, release the swing, make contact, and clobber the rawhide globe. Why not? After all, you taught him as much as he needed to master the skill of hitting a baseball. As the ball approaches, you are reasonably certain that all of those mechanics, so diligently rehearsed, will soon result in a glorious hit. But it does not. The athlete has a good stance in the batter's box, steps appropriately toward the ball, swings, and misses not once but three times. He strikes out. You watch your athlete walk dejectedly back to your dugout. What happens next? Do you get angry, react negatively toward the child, or do nothing?

First understand that what took place is not failure. It is feedback from the coaching messages that you sent. The message that you thought you sent was hit the ball. Your athlete listened and tried with varying levels of competence to respond to your message. During practice you implemented all of the best coaching that you could muster in the time available, and the result of that communication was a strikeout. Your athlete struck out for any number of reasons: athletic skill, understanding of what you were asking him to do, his physicality, competence with the technique of hitting, the ability of the pitcher, his grip on the bat, or simply nerves. To place blame, show impatience, or lose control of your emotions toward your athlete is counterproductive. Professional baseball hitters who fail to hit a ball 75 percent of the time earn millions of dollars for their effort. To be discouraged when your Little Leaguer misses the ball is foolish. Do not be discouraged, and do not personalize the event toward yourself or your athlete, but rather recognize what happened and let feedback guide your next step. You understand that what just happened resulted from the first two steps of communication—message sent and your athlete's receipt of that message—but the third step is the one that tells the tale. The key to turning your reaction to what takes place during competition into effective communication is the manner in which you respond to the actions and activity of your athletes. Take note of the feedback that you receive and let it guide your direction.

The Effect of Your Communication Is the Result You Achieve

Even though you thought you taught your athlete how to hit, dribble, catch a pass, take a shot on goal, or shoot a free throw, in reality they received only a portion of that message and were then only able to turn a still smaller portion of your message into physical skill. Growing athletic skill is a combination of intellectual comprehension and physical ability. Both take time, rehearsal, and effort. Improvement does not just happen. As the coach, go back to the first step; examine the message that you are sending. Start again. Go back to your workout and teach hitting again. You will do this for as long as you coach. Use all of the skills and techniques addressed in this book to patiently and consistently move your athletes to ever greater levels of skill. Always let feedback guide your direction. Communication is a cycle: sender, receiver, feedback, and return to sender. It is a continuing process. Each step contributes to the success of the whole. Constantly examine every step of the process, what you are doing, and how you can do it better. Improving your skills within those steps empowers you to turn coaching communication into an art form. I used baseball as my example here, but this technique works in any sport as you apply the principles outlined.

Just as a musician fine tunes their performance by listening to the playback from their concert performance, you advance your coaching to an ever improving state of competence and efficiency as you let feedback guide you. Don't think you can shortcut this process because you cannot. Coaching is a constantly evolving sequence of teaching, evaluating, working, and improving. If it is any comfort to you, as soon as your team starts to get it, the season will be over and you will start again next time with a new group of couch potatoes. Harold Burson, founding partner in the global PR firm Burson-Marseller, once said, "It is a good thing that communication is not a disease since we know so very little about it."[2]

Communication is a science, an art form, and a diminishing skill in our world of the constant mediated messages that are thrust upon us. We know how to send messages, but few know how to effectively or persuasively communicate. Better communication results from consistent application of the skills contained in this chapter.

You will never be a good coach or parent until you become an effective communicator, an interested listener, and a skilled questioner. Like every other valuable life skill, communication requires persistent application of principle.

2 Doug Newsom, Alan Scott, & Judy VanSlyke Turk. *This is PR: The Realities of Public Relations,* 4th Edition (California: Wadsworth Pub. 1989).

7

MAKE THEIR REASONS YOUR REASONS

Three Secrets to Motivating Young Athletes

One day in junior high school I entered a cross country race, placed second, and have never stopped running. I was the highest recruited athlete my senior year in a high school that produced a lot of athletic scholarship. Athletics paid for my education. Now that I am raising my children, I use my love of exercise to maintain personal balance.

—*Lida R., NJCAA National Champion Track and Field, All American Cross Country, NCAA Div. I All Region Track and Cross Country*

Thinking of motivation takes me back to the old-school mentalities that existed when I was in high school and college. Football, wrestling, track, and baseball were my sports. Even though I competed at varsity levels in all of these, I have no memory of my coaches ever talking about motivation. We were told to win. We wanted to win, but I don't remember any breakdown of goals, clarification of tasks, or any other coach-directed efforts to move me to greater performance, except yelling or not letting me play. Neither motivated me. The only motivating slogan I remember, if that is what it was, came from my high school assistant wrestling coach. Coach Garcia barked orders and pushed us through the hard work of wrestling while shouting the motivating encouragement of Vince Lombardi: "Winning isn't everything, it's the only thing."

I remember another: "Winning may not be the most important thing, but it is way ahead of whatever is in second place." I was certainly confused but not motivated at all.

If motivation means moving to new levels of commitment or effort, hearing these phrases did nothing for me. I continued working because that is what I knew I should do, but I thought nothing of these teaching or motivating moments as reasons for staying in my sport. Every Little League experience I recall as a child athlete centered on winning. Winning was the only goal (that and getting away from farm work). I remember no other value to sport than winning. But that was then and this is now. We coach in a different time. Winning is no longer a shared goal by every athlete and parent.

What Do We Do Today?

While you are a Little League coach, you will meet many parents who value teamwork, exercise, social skills, camaraderie, and involvement as much, if not more, than winning. If you disagree with that statement, get over it. If you cannot get over it, at least acknowledge it and know that there is more to winning than scores.

Enthusiastically declaring, "Let's win!" works for certain personalities but not for all. The participant on your team looking for the exercise or the participation doesn't care about winning. There are many reasons for playing Little League, so let's reexamine the process of motivation itself.

Motivating children requires a new paradigm. You always run the risk of damaging who your athletes are whenever you tell them who they are not. Consider your athletes in light of personality. By observing and noting their behavior within common interactions, it becomes possible to motivate in ways never used before. Building coaching dialogues that are constructed around these simple behavior-based models gives you a richness and confidence that you never had before. In this chapter we explore a process of motivating young athletes based on them rather than on you.

When Napoleon Hill published his landmark book *Think and Grow Rich* in 1937, the self-help industry began. To this day the foundation of helping one's self begins with attitude, "the starting point of all riches, whether they are riches of a material nature or intangible riches" (according to Napoleon Hill's own definition).[1] Positive Mental Attitude (PMA) is one of the more lasting theorems resulting from Hill's work and an important precursor to every action. PMA is a psychological state of mind capable of driving negative thinking from our psyche. While I believe that state of mind is important, the motivation process is more than attitude, particularly in young people. Too often we demand positive thinking from our athletes without a viable mechanism for moving personal behavior from that state of positive thought to the needed action that improves athletic performance.

The "What" to Do of Motivation

Step 1: Thought

Thought is an intellectual recognition of something that should be done, a direction that ought to be taken or a behavior that needs to change. Whether positive or negative, thought is the first component of motivation. Your athletes usually come to Little League with good attitudes and positive thoughts toward their involvement with the sport. They want to be there and have fun, which is the beginning of your work. You must move them to action. Action moves your athlete toward their best experience and propels your coaching to its most successful conclusions.

Step 2: Belief

Belief is a conviction that you can take action upon a thought. Your kids are learning how to believe in themselves. In order to motivate them, you must assist them in making the connection between what they think (their intellectual recognition) and what they believe (their personal conviction to act upon thought). Your coaching moves them to that greater effort when you implement effective strategies and use the skills you are about to learn.

---

1 Napoleon Hill, Think and Grow Rich (New York: Fawcett Books, 1987).

Step 3: Action!

Clint Eastwood has a list of ten things he believes are critical to success. The most impressive item on the list is to keep moving. Consider this counsel in light of your team. In order to effect change, you must move from the place where you are now to the place where you want to be. As a coach, you intellectually recognize what needs to be done, believe in your personal skills to take action, and keep moving. You must guide your athletes through all three steps.

I always felt something was missing from established motivational thinking. My search for the missing link to motivation began more than thirty years ago in Canada. For two years I taught the native Canadian children. I had a companion in this effort by the name of Palmer. He decided one day that we were just not doing things correctly, so he made an attempt to motivate me and our staff by hanging a huge sign for all to see. I am certain he was reading Napoleon Hill at the time. The sign read simply, "PMA." A few of the children in our school saw the large letters hanging on the wall. Not knowing how to react, they simply asked, "What does PMA mean?"

Before we could give an explanation, one of the children volunteered, "Palmer's mad again?"

That experience was a great example of my partner talking at rather than to someone. I never found his PMA proclamation as a reason to do or act better, and neither did the children. When you add thirty years of increasingly brassy attitudes in children and adolescent cynicism, finding a motivation solution that actually works becomes challenging. Today's child is often apathetic, physically unskilled, and elsewhere engaged. Maxims such as "quitters never win" and "winners never quit" or any number of the tried and true motivational phrases are often disregarded and many times counterproductive. But this question still remains: How do I motivate athletes?

The Secret—Motivation Comes from Them

Three personalities are apparent on any Little League team. By understanding a few simple behaviors that each member of your team exhibits, it becomes possible to affect their attitude and move them toward improved action. Rather than hope that some pithy comment will be so powerful in the arrangement of its words that all listeners are moved in a prescribed direction, you can improve your coaching by speaking to the personality of each member of your team in a voice that they individually recognize and accept.

Speak in Their Voice—Not Your Own

In the next few pages, I will show you how to speak in a voice that motivates young people, produces speech constructs that are capable of creating new attitudes in your athletes, and connects positive action like nothing you have ever used before. The gateway to motivation opens through a framework of your athlete's personal behaviors, which are natural and observable conditions. You are about to learn a new coaching tool. As you connect the behavior and natural tendencies of athletes to your new way of speaking, an exciting new world opens for you. Speaking through this behaviorally directed voice correlates attitude with action. Coaching becomes effective and motivation real because you no longer employ force of will, anger, or guilt to create change. Athletes motivate themselves because through your voice they are hearing their own.

Motivation—the How-to-Do

If you are a happy person and smile and laugh, I do not have to motivate you to smile or laugh. I just let you do it. If you love to compete, I do not have to move you to a love of competition; I simply manage an environment that gives you opportunity to compete. If you love pizza and are hungry, motivating you to eat pizza is easy. I simply provide pizza.

Rather than approaching motivation as a *reason* for behavior, look at it as the *result* of behavior. Motivation occurs; it is a natural by-product when you match their reasons to engage with the activities that you coach. Motivation is not manipulation. Manipulation is the sheer force of my will upon yours until you do what I want you to do. Motivation and manipulation are as different as winning and losing, with an even larger distinction between the two. One represents free choice, the other does not. When you manipulate, you engage athletes for your reasons. When motivated, they engage in action because of their own self-interest. Motivational coaching occurs when I respect my athlete enough to recognize his or her natural personality and speak in the same voice of that personality. As you use this new way of speaking, your athletes find reasons to engage and take action toward a goal. As you articulate and share goals, meaningful elements begin to emerge and are shared by both of you as you engage in the team and sport experience.

A team may have a purpose to play better at the end of the season than at the beginning because of their shared meaning for taking part in the league, and each member of the team will have a personal reason for fulfilling that purpose. Purposes may include gaining skill, getting exercise, winning games, having fun, all of the above, or something else. The reason for a purpose is to articulate a shared vision between the athletes and coaches and establish why you want to accomplish that purpose. Motivation comes from finding connections between personal needs that must be met and the shared meaning of that team's purpose. Your job is to connect personal reasons with purpose. As you do, you motivate your players.

Yeah right! That's as close to psychobabble as I get. But I know what I am talking about, and I am certain it will work for you because it works for me every day. Now let me show you how to motivate young couch potatoes as well.

Beginning

Motivation is the reason you or an athlete engages in action, abides by rules of the team, justifies technical work, or charts plans for competitive success. Participation that matches with innate personality needs will produce motivation. Speaking in the voice that is recognized by your athletes' natural personality requires that you intelligently manage your thoughts and conversations.

When you speak to your athlete in a voice that drives natural behavior, you base conversations on things that they naturally seek. Recognizing personal behaviors and speaking to your athlete with the appropriate voice matches reason with action. Motivation happens. Motivation is always a by-product of a quality relationship between coach and athlete. Giving your athletes a reason to perform is never a battle of ego or will but rather a directive from shared purpose wherein athletes motivate themselves because you speak to them in terms of who they are, rather than what you want them to be.

Know Who They Are

Begin by understanding your athletes. Each is different and motivated by separate behaviors. In my experience, I can point to three distinct personalities that exist on any team. I refer to them as Team Leaders, Team Members, and Teammates. Each is motivated by personal behaviors that are naturally a part of them but which connect in varying degrees with the Little League experience. Your success depends on how effectively you match their personal behavioral needs with your team's purpose.

- Team Leaders are motivated by opportunity.
- Team Members are motivated by process.
- Teammates are motivated by recognition.

In the next few pages, I will show you how to understand your athletes in the context of these three distinct and separate personality types, employ a few simple strategies that will recognize those behaviors, and then incorporate your observation of who they naturally are and engage these behaviors in your coaching. Giving them what they naturally seek creates motivation powerful enough to create the change that you want. Because you are giving them reasons to act in a way that best serves your team and their interests, improvement and commitment become a natural occurrence within your program.

A Word of Clarification

Do not confuse Team Leader with the person who serves as your team captain. The team captain is the designated player you rely on to call kids for changes in practice times, remind someone of treats, gather equipment, and perform other helpful tasks. A team captain is a young assistant coach and comes from any of these three behaviors.

Recognizing Your Team

Team Leaders are competitive, dominant, assertive, independent, sometimes arrogant, usually self-assured, and always looking for opportunities to compete. They want control of their own activities and seek every opportunity to prove themselves in competition and independence.

Team Members are quiet, thoughtful, organized, and diligent. They love to work at the game and want details from you about the game. They want to know what to do, how to do it, and time and support in experimenting with it. They are the question askers because the final outcome of the game or workout depends on the process. They will ask for your help because they do what you ask them to do. Their commitment to process is so great that any failure will be the result of your coaching, rather than their effort. Team Members give you all they have.

Teammates are happy, talkative, and everyone's friend. They are outgoing, welcome new kids quickly, and remain optimistic when things go wrong. They love to hear their name and be recognized for what they do. Teammates want to be liked and want everyone to like them back. It is important to a Teammate that each member of the team feels liked by everyone else.

Behavior Reveals Itself—If You Watch

Suppose you are coaching a Little League football team. You gather the group around you and say, "The first one to the fence and back is the winner."

The Team Leader is gone before you can finish your statement because all she wants is an opportunity to compete. Given that opportunity, she motivates herself. You do nothing except provide the setting for opportunity. You motivate Team Leaders by giving them freedom to act independently and opportunity to prove themselves.

Your Team Members will run to the fence and back, but they want more detail: how fast to run, whether they need to touch the fence or just run past it, whether they need to do other exercises along the way. You motivate them by giving them the details of the process. You cannot punish them for errors because any errors are a result of your coaching. You always point them toward the quality of the workout and why drills and effort grow competence. They love the process and will buy into your organization.

The Teammates want to be seen running to the fence. They will talk all the way there and back and keep talking after they return. The Teammates are the happy ones, the jokers, the talkers, everybody's best friend. You motivate them with status and prestige. Let them lead the warm-ups, tell others what to do, or build agreement among the rest of the team. They are motivated by social interaction, acceptance, and recognition.

At the end of a game, the Team Leaders are looking forward to the next game, the Team Members are anxious to fix any problems in practice, and the Teammates want to tell everyone about the game.

A Scouting Example

I am a Boy Scout leader and have a Teammate in my troop. He is a bright young man and talks all the time. He is the only boy I ever met who can eat while talking. Food going in literally passes words coming out of his mouth. After he missed a recent campout, my scoutmaster and I were talking about how to motivate him to greater attendance in troop activities. I shared these theories of Team Leader, Team Member, and Teammate. We decided to speak to this scout in his voice (Teammate). The next time I saw him I said, "Where were you? We missed you. You have to go with us on the next campout."

He asked why.

I said, "Because if you do not go, then we have no stories. You are the best storyteller in the troop."

He was on the next scout trip, and we could not shut him up.

A Team and Personal Victory Example

My varsity wrestling team was in a building year. We were young and competing in a tough region. We were wrestling one of our strongest rivals, a team we had never beaten before. My guys did a great job and with one match left, the score was us thirty-one to their thirty-two. Winning one more match would do the unbelievable. We could win the dual meet. My last athlete to compete was a Team Member. If he won his match, we would win the dual meet contest. If he lost, then the whole team lost. This kind of pressure is tough for any athlete. The crowd was into the match. The rest of the team was screaming, and he was nervous. I could have easily missed motivating him to be successful during this critical moment, but I knew who he was and I knew how to talk to him in his own voice.

Had my athlete been a Team Leader, I would have said, "You win this match, we win the dual. Get it done and don't hurt him." Had he been a Teammate, I would have said, "When you win, they will talk about you all day tomorrow." He would have given his best effort because he would have wanted the recognition that I had just described.

But my athlete was a Team Member, motivated by process. Hard work meant something to him. He drew his reasons for succeeding from effort and drill because they were the process of athletic training. I said, "No worries. All you do is wrestle the same way you have been practicing. Your preparation has been exceptional. There is no way that you will lose because you are going to wrestle the way you prepared. I have seen it all week long. Just out work him." He walked out and won by a technical fall, scoring fifteen points more than his opponent. We won the match by a score of thirty-six to thirty-two.

How to Identify Your Athletes

Watch your athletes. As you get to know them, work out with them, and guide them through competition. Notice how they respond to each other and any given situation. Play a game, something not associated with your sport with loosely defined rules. You can play keep-away with a soccer ball, touch football, tag, or even take them swimming and allow creative play. Watch how they behave in neutral settings. Who immediately moves quickly to score to take control of the game? Who is smiling and wants to stay on the sideline and talk? Who is constantly asking for a clarification of the rules? Who is declaring new rules? Who is quiet? Who is vocal when they are not the center of the action? Remember, the Team Leader wants to be dominant, assertive, and competitive. The Team Member wants process, rules, formality, and clarification of what happens now and what happens later. The Teammate wants to have fun, talk about it, and tell everyone else about it.

Sculpt individual conversations, incorporating the behavior of each athlete. Base everything around your personality observations. Remember what your athlete needs and then support that behavior in practice, in conversation, and during competition. You are motivating them because you are giving them what they naturally seek and want to do. Motivation is not a result of you forcing your will. Most of today's kids will rebel long before submitting to your will. Motivation occurs within a framework of relationship guided by your understanding of who they are and their personal need.

An Important Note

You are observing behaviors. There is no right or wrong to a behavior. One is not more important than the other. Everyone has a varying proportion of each of these three behaviors in their personality, but one of the three will take precedence over the others. You are recognizing a natural condition that exists within a continuum of intensity. The more an athlete displays a particular behavior, the more they respond to its satisfaction. One behavior will be more pronounced than the others. Recognizing each behavior is the basis of using these simple techniques to motivate young athletes.

An athlete who is very competitive and has no time for drills because they only want to win has one behavior more prevalent: Team Leader. You coach that athlete by teaching them that drills produce a greater ability to win. Even better, design competitive drills for your Team Leader. Give them an opportunity to compete in drills, strength training, or conditioning.

Teammates are happy. Let them talk, within reason. I have seen coaches who fight to keep kids quiet. We tell them to be quiet, and they don't like that because they are not doing what they are naturally motivated to do. Let them talk. Do not be afraid to recognize them when they say something. You cannot let them take over, but you cannot shut them out either. It is counterproductive for a coach to take away their motivation and still expect them to perform. I can stop by any Little League practice field today, regardless of the sport, and watch coaches stifle their athlete's personal and behavioral reasons for participating on that team. And while that the coach is turning off their reasons for performing, he is frustrated by their lack of performance. It is like pushing gas and brake pedals at the same time and wondering why the car does not move.

A Word of Caution

You as the coach are also a Team Member, Team Leader, or Teammate. Be wise as you interact with your athletes. It is easy to create huge personality issues with the kids you coach. You need to be smart enough to recognize and then modify your own behavior. If you are a Team Leader and send a Team Member into the game using your Team Leader voice, he will not be motivated. But if you speak his language and say,

"This is why we did that drill yesterday and all you have to do is what you did during practice," he will hear that and respond to it. He will put forth his best effort and gain confidence because you are giving him the information he needs. The more certainty you give your Team Member, the more he or she will respond. Let them know that what they do every day matters. Let them know why you do a particular drill or how that skill improves them. Always give them time to train, try, and work. Plan your workouts down to the details of how much time is allowed for drinks.

If you are a Teammate, the most important thing for you is being the center of the fun and making sure everyone has a good time. You will also spend too much time talking to your team. While you will have a great time, your kids will be challenged to improve. Your Team Leader will not care about the happy talk. Your Team Member will not try because there is no process. If you, the coach, are a Team Leader and you are coaching a Teammate, she will want to talk and be recognized, and her talk will annoy you. As a result of your behavior colliding with hers, her motivation will wane until she simply stops responding to you. She is not going to like you. In fact she will think you are annoying because every time she says something you stop her and assert yourself. You are always caught between what she craves and what you demand. Turn it around. If you were being coached and your natural assertive behavior (Team Leader) was being circumvented by a talkative coach (Teammate) or a process oriented coach (Team Member), you would be frustrated as well.

Add the fact that today's kids know how to cut noise out of their world, and you see how fast and possible it is to become nothing more than a tinkling bell or a brass band with no tune. Your athletes stop responding. You yell more. They block it out. Not only is motivation destroyed, but communication disappears as well. Pay attention to who they are and get comfortable with the personalities of the kids in front of you. Understand the three personalities swirling around you. Start talking to them in the voice that they want to hear and modify your own voice accordingly. You are the adult. As you make changes, they will respond. Give them settings and scenarios where the things that matter to them are present in your training, coaching dialogue, workout, administration, and everything that you do. You will find that kids are motivated to step up and perform for you. You will also have a great time.

A Team Member Example

I coached a boy who was not very athletic on my wrestling team. You will hardly ever find a greater kid, a better worker, or a finer young man. During his junior year he struggled. We suggested that he get involved in some off-season wrestling by joining a junior Olympic club. He did and worked hard but was not having much success from a win-loss standpoint. However, the added work was indeed making him a better wrestler. The State Club Championships were the final competition of the season. It was to be his last event, with the exception of summer camp, until fall and his senior year. In spite of working hard and getting better, he lost two matches and was out of the tournament. His work ethic was exceptional, so he was pretty frustrated, even to the point of tears, because, if he had 10 percent more natural athleticism, we would have seen a much greater improvement in his skills.

I knew he was a Team Member, and I certainly did not want him to be so frustrated that we lost him. I was certain that he would have a lot of success his senior year. I spoke to him in a Team Member voice: "I am so proud of how hard you are working. I know you cannot tell right now, but I promise you that what you are doing is going to pay off. When we get to the season next fall, you are going to win a lot of matches."

That meant a lot to him. He told me later that it gave him the confidence and motivation to stay with us one more year. He went to the summer camp. He was elected team captain and won the majority of his matches during the season. Several of his wins were critical and helped us have an undefeated season for the first time in our region competitions.

The difference between where he was as a sophomore and where he ended his senior year was like night and day. He persevered because the process meant something to him. He was a huge strength to our program. Did he win every match? No. Did he make a difference for us many times? Absolutely. Did his example and commitment to work make a difference for us in the room as a part of practice? Every day! His commitment to process gave us a great peer mentor. Because he loved drills, working, and process, his leadership example fed into the younger boys. They saw what it means to work. They noticed how he responded to challenges. Even though he was hardly ever in the championships, he was always in the competition.

I'm not sure what would have happened if I had I coached him as a Team Leader. But I do know that he would have easily shut out my assertive voice. He felt bad enough about not winning more than two matches during the state championships. Getting better could have easily been turned off all together. The Teammate voice would have meant nothing to him either because recognition did not motivate him. He cared about process. I was grateful to understand a structure that helped us both through a difficult moment and continued his high school career. He blessed himself and he blessed our team.

A Team Leader Example

My former college teammate is a successful coach who has led a competitive program, one of the best in the state, for twenty-five years. He coaches a powerful Team Leader, whom I will call John. John is a three-time state champion and a four-time national champion. Following the weigh-in for a Junior Olympic tournament, John returned to my friend to report that he was wrestling a weight higher than his actual weight. When asked why, John said, "There are seven state champions in the heavier weight. I am the only one in my weight."

John saw an opportunity to compete against seven state champions and jumped at the chance. The only coaching he needed when he saw this opportunity was to stay out of his way and let him go. His impressive accomplishments indicate that he is a winner. But why? For him, it is because he loves to compete. John is a Team Leader and completely motivated by any opportunity to assert and test himself.

Raising responsible children assures the future of society. The future stability of our community requires that we teach our children how to accept challenges, give of themselves to a greater good, and stay their course with tenacity and courage.

8

WINNING WITHOUT SCORING

Three Coaching Strategies That Build Success

I found my love of teaching while assisting Coach Clapier in a junior high program. We taught athletes how to succeed and thrive in tough situations. Twelve years later, I am a turn-around specialist for our state board of education. I go into failing schools to raise cultural and performance standards. Coach Mike taught me that kids respond to structure, encouragement, and concern.

—*Matt M., Educator, Vice Principal, and Former Assistant Coach*

I WENT TO DINNER WITH a good friend the other night. He is retired from coaching after nearly thirty years of working with kindergarten through high school athletes. We talked about the philosophy of coaching and the good and bad coaches we have known. Our discussion centered on one coach in particular who created a strong high school program at the expense of balance. Winning is so important to him that he imports athletes from other schools, even other states, to support his winning ways. This practice of recruiting elite athletes from outside the physical boundary of local schools grows every day. His program has many good features. It is a varsity program rather than Little League, so winning has greater weight. But his focus is so concentrated on winning that others notice. I asked my friend the difference between this program and the one he managed. He said simply, "I was in the business of building boys and he is not."

Winning is a by-product of a good program. It is not the focus, especially in Little League. If you are teaching skills and preparing your athletes for sustained improvement in the sport, you will see many successful outcomes during competition, including owning more points than your opponent when time runs out. But if winning is your primary purpose and victory your ultimate goal, you will find yourself out of balance sooner rather than later. The list of horrible things done in the name of winning is long when parents, coaches, and athletes count winning by the score of competition as the only reason for participation. Here are some examples:

- A baseball coach in Florida attacks an umpire, and the choke hold that he has on the ump's neck must forcefully be removed by others over a call made during a girls T-ball game.
- A Little League football game in Pennsylvania turns into a brawl involving more than one hundred parents, coaches, and fans.
- Two mothers of high school baseball players in Utah disagree with a call and end up in a gunfight in the parking lot. One dies.

What Is Your Philosophy?

A coach's personal philosophy is easily apparent by what he does. Watch him in action. Here's an example: Several innings into a baseball game, the Little League Yankees were leading. While chasing a fly ball to short left field, the opposing third baseman and left fielder crashed together. The injury was bad. An eleven-year-old boy lay on the field with a broken leg. The game was stopped, and an ambulance took the boy to the hospital. But caring for the boy took a lot of time. The field had no lights. As darkness approached, we knew that finishing the game in the dwindling daylight would be impossible. The coach of the injured player approached the coach of the Yankees and asked when to reschedule the remaining couple of innings. "There is no need to do that," was his reply. "We're ahead now and you won't catch us, so this game is over. There is no need to play the remaining innings."

Why not? Weren't they there to give the kids an opportunity to play? In one moment this coach revealed his personal coaching philosophy. He was there to add one more "W" to his win/loss record. There was no need to finish the game. The coach of the injured boy even offered to count the game a Yankee win but play the remaining innings. What harm could come from that? But those innings were never played. The Yankees counted the game as a win. The young boy with the broken leg recovered, and a coach who valued winning more than kids revealed himself through less than admirable behavior.

What Drives Your Program?

A quality program creates a vibrant working balance between physical effort and personal improvement. The coach's philosophy determines the quality of the program and defines its accomplishment. Coaching's measure of success is greater than win/loss records because your influence goes far beyond the playing field. Long after the game is forgotten, it is who you were and what you taught your kids that remain. A coach's effect and influence is limitless and can work either for good or for ill.

Three coaching strategies direct the actions of coaching in a quality program. You will note the absence of winning as a singular objective. Achieving desired goals and meaning is the direct result of mastering these three ways of doing. The three keys are validate progress, connect with potential, and assure future action.

1. Validate Progress

Lacking a clear destination, one road is just as good as another. Give your athletes a place to go so they can know their place during the journey.

When my sons entered junior high school, I volunteered to coach their wrestling team. I had not coached at that level since my older son was a member of the same team about ten years before. On the first day of practice, I declared a vision for the team. I told them that they were going to be the best varsity team the high school ever had. At the time, we were in transition at the varsity level. Our coach of twenty years was retiring, and we were beginning a new era with a new coach. I then placed a sign over the door into our practice room that simply stated: "Through these doors walk the finest junior high school wrestlers in our district." It is a custom to end practice with a cheer. Our high school mascot is the Eagle. At the end of every practice, we spelled E-A-G-L-E and shouted "Eagle!" We called it "eagle out." It was one way of reinforcing who we were and where we were going. This story is still developing since about half of this team is in high school, but last season we were the best dual team in the history of our school, having gone undefeated in our varsity region.

Ask yourself the following questions:

- What is your vision for the program?
- Is it written and shared with your athletes and their parents?
- Do you consistently confirm that vision?

Components of a Vision Statement

A quality vision statement will do the following:

- Be simple to repeat.
- Be easy to understand.
- Validate every member of your program.
- Create a shared direction for the season.
- Articulate achievable goals.

Your vision statement becomes your point of reference for the work that you do. If my Little League vision statement was to have fun, learn skills, and play baseball again next year, I would have a point of reference for everything that we did. I would constantly check with athletes to make sure that they were having fun. I would do a skill assessment early in the season to see what they could do and what they could not do. As we worked and they improved, I would point out improvements on an individual level for each kid. When you play in a game, it is more important that you assess their ability based on skill rather than outcome of competition.

A baseball player who strikes out when a hit would serve the team better should be spoken to like this: "That was one of the best ups that you've had. You really are watching the ball and swinging the best you have all year." Dialogue such as this builds confidence and improvement as it validates progress. During your next practice, continue to build on these physical skills using the ACRE method.

2. Connect with Potential

In the movie *Saving Private Ryan,* a squad of soldiers is sent on a dangerous mission—find one man and remove him from harm's way during the invasion of France. In a war movie, danger is apparent, and understanding the worth of one person is easy to comprehend. The athletes on your team are not facing danger like Private Ryan's, but how important are they to you? Measure the worth of your young athletes by their potential. This is a serious responsibility. Coaching places you in a very important relationship whether you want it or not. How you handle your responsibility will have more impact than you know. That impact can be for as much bad as it is for good.

I asked a twelve-year-old boy how he liked Little League football and his should-a-been coach.

"He just yelled all the time," was his reply.

"Are you going to play again this year?" I asked.

"No way."

"Why not?"

"I hated it."

"What did you want?"

"I wanted to have fun and learn how to play football."

The boy is now out of the sport and says he will not play again. Because he was coached by a man with poor coaching skills, a winning-matters-most-mentality, and an inability to respect what the kids wanted, this young man's future possibility within football is gone.

A measurement of value in the advertising business is the reach of a particular medium. Reach is how many people will read the newspaper, hear the radio show, or watch the Super Bowl. Millions of dollars are spent on understanding media's ability to reach the desired audience. What is your reach as a coach? How far will your influence be felt, and what will be said about your tenure? Your time with the athlete is short in terms of their entire life. If you coach a child for one Little League baseball season, you will see them for a few hours. But if you start a group of soccer players at six and stay with them until high school, you can become a close ally, confidante, and mentor. You can also become ineffective, nonessential, or even harmful. The difference between outcomes is measured by your respect for their potential and your ability to help them reach it.

Kids you coach must know that they are capable of more than they can do right now and that you believe they will grow and improve. Validate them. Assure them. Coach them. They will believe in themselves when you first believe in them. Measure them against a belief in what they can become rather than their ability to win a game for you today.

Each Athlete Is Valuable

I coached a neighborhood Little League baseball team for two years. We used a county recreational facility with a gorgeous view of the valley and spent many great afternoons and evenings watching our kids play ball. Most of us valued our boys' experiences more than winning, but we had a coach who placed winning above everything.

Our local league rule was to not start a new inning after an hour and forty-five minutes. We did this so that we could get more games in even though the rules clearly indicate that a game consists of a minimum of five complete innings. We were playing a game against this coach, whom I'll call Warren, on his home field. We were the second game of the day against his team. He won the first, and we played a very tight game against him until the fourth inning. When the inning ended, we had played one hour and fifty minutes. According to the rule we had used for two years, the game should have been over and my team should've won because we were ahead by one run. But Coach Warren held up a rule book and said, "The rules state a complete game is five innings. We've only played four. We play one more inning."

We played the final inning. He got the runs that he needed and won the game. My assistant coach and I were perplexed because we had always adhered to the time limit. I did not fully understand how important winning was to Coach Warren until I found out that in the game before ours he was ahead when the time limit expired. Coach Warren then insisted that the time limit be imposed and would not allow a new inning to start. Over the course of two games, he worked the same rule in opposite ways; both to his advantage, both with an end to winning the game for his team.

We had other problems in this league. Coach Warren's wife was also the league administrator. She did not use certified umpires. Both of those issues were soon resolved because this nonsense of manipulating rules had gone too far. But the real damage was done. Six years later when my kids graduated from high school, they still remembered Coach Warren. He moved away from our town but was always remembered as a cheater. To this day, nearly twenty years later, athletes from that team remember him as a man with no honor. This story represents one of the first times that I watched Little League coaches reveal themselves through the prism of young people's athletics. I was amazed, infuriated, and saddened at the same time. The crazy does not stop there. This league had another coach with a similar obsession for winning. He was not above brush backs, taunts, or intentionally hitting players with pitches. At the end of the season, this pathetic pair got into a fight about whose team had the better record. Unable to accept anything other than win-at-all-cost, they each bought separate trophies and declared themselves the champion.

Neither of these coaches ever produced a high school player. The naturally gifted athletes were pushed hard and burnt out by the time they reached high school's varsity level. They lacked humility, commitment, and work ethic that is necessary to improve and get to the next level. The player who seldom played was never taught to work or allowed to improve. Skills were not developed for everyone within the construct of each practice. Either the kids could play or they could not. These coaches won using existing skill levels of children and failed to help their athletes develop physical skills, individual ethics, or personal love for the game. Most of these players stopped playing baseball following that season, except the sons of the should-a-been coaches, but both were out of baseball before high school.

3. *Assure Future Success*

I grew up in Idaho and spent a couple of weeks every year on the South Fork of the Salmon River. It was paradise. The fish were plentiful and the mountains challenging. My brothers and I were free. One day we decided to climb the tallest mountain, Pilot's Peak.

Mountain tops are sacred places. These climbs taught me reverence for the task and appreciation for the vision falling away before my feet. I have always loved standing on the top of mountains. The climb is difficult and humbling—difficult because of the physical effort required to get there and humbling because in the Idaho primitive area taking that final step to reach the summit reveals thousands of similar peaks just as high as the one you worked all day to conquer.

The view from the top of Pilot's Peak is spectacular. To the west across the drainage of the South Fork is a spectacular mountain. A road drops off the top and winds its way across a huge clear portion of sage brush and pine before forking several times as it descends to the river miles below. Life's journey mirrors those mountain pathways. It has roads we must decide to travel, changing conditions that affect us, and choices that take us to a variety of destinations.

If you have not already done so, you need to ask why you are involved in youth sports. One reason is to win games by coaching children. As I am sure you know by now, that is only one reason. We are here to instill a love for the sport, a capacity for physical work, and an experience within the camaraderie of friends and opponents. Youth sport is a healthy activity worth doing in and of itself. We are not training kids for professional careers. The odds of one of your athletes becoming a professional athlete are many thousands to one. However, the odds of your athlete becoming a successful person, contributing citizen, and healthy adult are nearly assured. You can even wager money that the kids you coach will become adults who will view their time with you in some context. Great youth coaches are remembered and revered. If you are a poor coach, they will hardly recall your name. They will, however, remember how their experience with you hurt them.

Coaches and youth athletics create a foundation for success in life. Paul Johnson reports in *Modern Times* that the battles of Waterloo were won on the playing fields of Seton. Some of our kids will become warriors, some teachers, some even coaches. I have several former athletes serving in the military from Army Ranger to Air Force Physician. I count doctors, lawyers, business professionals, craftsmen, and more among my former athletes. The majority of the children we coach will become responsible adults. As a coach, you will always play an important part in that development. One of my finest life-affirming moments is being out in public and hearing a voice call, "Coach." It is a rich but brief moment that sanctions a relationship shared years before.

Consider all that you can contribute to their lives while grooming athletic skills, personal accountability, responsibility, self-worth, confidence, a capacity for work, social interactions, and a discovery of what they may be and who they might become. Connect them to that future success rather than rob them of even the smallest part of their potential. Give them a safe place, a good working environment where they can simply be themselves, have fun, and learn. Let the athletes you coach try harder than they did before, go farther, and become better than they ever thought possible before they met you

Even a Bad Example Offers a Teaching Moment

I watched a Little League football coach tell a number of ten-year-old kids not to sign up for Little League because there was no way they could compete with "his" boys. In this particular league, as is the custom in most programs, there is a must-play rule—every participant plays at least ten plays during each game. This coach felt that he could not win the league championship unless he kept his best players on the field at all times. He knew his core of good athletes and did not want to make room for players whose skills, size, or speed were not on the same level as the players on his team. He would not chance reducing his winning percentages. His priority was weeding out unknown talent, giving them no chance, no help, and no thanks. The league required that teams split and form second teams when too many athletes registered. Accommodating the must-play rule was difficult when the size of the teams grew beyond twenty. A split was mandatory at thirty-two kids. This team was stuck in that awkward place with not enough kids to split the team and too many to keep the favored players on the field most of the time. Winning was more important than participation to this coach. When the kids were encouraged not to play or to quit, they listened.

Six years later, a team of that age group needed new players to fill a high school roster. But the boys who were turned away from Little League were gone. They were playing other sports or had lost interest in sports completely. Because of an overbearing focus on winning, this Little League program denied participation to some, limited potential for others, and failed to produce the high school players they might have had on their team if every child had been given an equal opportunity to participate. The final gut-wrench of the experience is that several of the kids who were discouraged to play grew larger and faster than the kids who were part of the coach's favored group. They found involvement in healthy physical activity through other sports, but they never returned to football. This age group was the smallest in number of any group to ever enter our high school. The damage done by this coach reached one more low point. When his son reached high school, they left the school fed by our Little League team and enrolled in a neighboring school. Only time will tell what his coaching meant to the program, but right now this group is entering its second year of high school and more boys are gone than remain.

Was this a deliberate effort to undermine a development program? Was he just a poor coach? Was he doing what he honestly thought best for the athletes? Whatever the case, bad examples that define wrongful behavior can point to better processes. Use them. In conclusion, let me share a comment from George F. Will's brilliant baseball book, *Men at Work*: "Greek philosophers considered sport a religious and civic—in a word, moral—undertaking. Sport, they said is morally serious because mankind's noblest aim is the loving contemplation of worthy things, such as beauty and courage. By witnessing physical grace, they should come to understand and love beauty. Seeing people compete courageously and fairly helps emancipate the individual by educating his passions."[1]

Oh, that youth sport and its coaches could assimilate that philosophy. I found this quote on the wall of a school gymnasium. It represents to me how far we have come in moving the play opportunities of our children from spontaneity to structure. There are many reasons we must always keep children under observation, but there is a sadness that attends our time as well. The innocence of youth and its attendant quickness for creative play is being diminished

1 George F. Will, *Men at Work* (New York: Harber PB, March 15, 1991).

While coaching, I seek every opportunity to let our workouts and time together be fun. Yes, there is a time for structure, but there is a paucity of free wheeling play among children. As coaches, it is our responsibility to return the play into a safe structure designed within the constructs of our Little Leagues.

9

DESIGNING EFFECTIVE WORKOUTS

Three Secrets to Leave Kids Tired and Eager for More

I immigrated to America in my early teens. I walked into Coach Mike's workout and found a home among brothers. I am from a single child Chinese family. I learned a love for hard work, physical exercise, and how to finish the season or task—skills that serve me well while earning graduate honors while earning my master's degree in accounting. My future is unlimited.

—*Haoran J., Magna Cum Laude, Master's Degree in Accounting*

My daughter holds the 5K and 10K school records at Utah State University. During her career, she was a national champion, all-region team member, and academic All-American. I say that partly to brag but also as an introduction to the overlooked topic of how you design your workout. She began running in junior high school and then consistently competed for the next ten years, while earning the above mentioned distinctions as well as her degree. In speaking with her about athletic preparation for competition, she emphasized the importance of the warm-up period, the place where every workout begins. While in high school she fought a consistent battle between passing time before the race and dealing with her nerves. Her coach told her to stop worrying and start warming up. It prepared her for the race and dispelled her nervousness. She became such a fan of the warm-up that her college teammates accused her of spending too much time preparing.

The converse of that story is the Little League football player who tells me he does not want to warm up because he is saving his energy for the game, or the baseball players who jog around the field once and call it good. They think they are warm and ready to play, but they are not. Three secrets to creating an effective workout are as follows:

1. Movement before stretching
2. Organized and planned activity based on needed skills
3. Make the ending fun

During an effective workout you will move your athletes through these elements:

- Warm up with agilities
- Stretch
- Technique, skill, and drills
- Game or competition situations
- Live play
- Conditioning
- Cool down and stretch
- Fun

1. Movement Before Stretching

Warm Up with Agilities

The order of the workout can vary, except for the first two components; you must warm up before stretching. Blood must flow to the muscles before stretching begins. I cringe whenever I see a team stretching without first warming up. Some coaches will take their team them on a short jog before the stretch, but even that overlooks an important period of time for developing physicality.

I begin every workout by exercising large muscles and elevating breathing (cardio). Jogging or tossing a ball or Frisbee are good activities, as long as you move long enough to quicken the pulse. The purpose is to get bodies moving and blood flowing without working anything too strenuously. As your players get warm, increase the intensity of the exercise by adding sport-specific movements that focus on big muscle movement. Your warm-up is complete when athletes are sweating and breathing hard.

If I am coaching baseball, I start with a jog. Sometimes I give each kid a ball and have them run in pairs and toss the ball back and forth as they run. Active stretching includes leg kicks, striders, and up and down motion to help build hip strength. The core of the human body is neglected by our sedentary lifestyles. Sit-ups, push-ups, crab crawls, bear crawls, up and down level changes of hips, and lunges are all good. Any sport-specific skill is excellent. I also count slow sprinting, somersaults, forward rolls, backward rolls, tumbling, and other general movements as part of the warm-up. You can always have your athletes run a ten- or fifteen-yard sprint, but keep it slow. Start from a stance position and run. As they warm up, increase the intensity but never reach an all-out effort until stretching is complete. The younger the athlete, the more general the warm-up should be. Let the core of the body guide your exercises. Develop what they do not develop in their own play with an eye to the specific needs of your sport. Years ago kids ran on the playgrounds of our schools. That may not be true today. The hours that kids used to spend in physical activity are now destroyed by electronic activity. While video games are great for hand-eye coordination, they are a disaster for lungs, backs, and muscles.

The Fatigue Wall

Kids today do not know how to push through the fatigue wall. They will resist warming up because they think it makes them tired and leaves them unable to compete. Of course, this is not true. You will coach kids who have never pushed through the fatigue wall to discover their own strength and abundant energy waiting on the other side. Our kids are so physically pampered that most do not know what they are capable of doing. You might be the first person to push them hard enough to sweat, ache, or hurt. After you move through the large muscle warm-up, put your team through pertinent sport agilities. Then give them a five-minute water break and reassemble for stretching.

Stretching

Stretching time is not visiting time. The biggest mistake I see, especially with younger kids who don't know how to stretch, is that coaches use stretch time as their own preparation time. While coaches discuss what they will do in practice, the kids attempt to stretch. This is an easy trap to fall into. You must oversee stretching. If you have enough staff, assign one coach to oversee stretching. If you do not have the assistants, you must prepare your practice content before practice and be present while your team stretches.

Muscles are like rubber bands and must be pulled in order to strengthen, lengthen, and avoid injury. Correct stretching is uncomfortable and requires effort.

Find a Dancer

One of the best things that I have done for a team is to have a dancer show us how to stretch. Ask a parent or friend with a background in dancing to take twenty minutes at the beginning of a workout and show your athletes what it really takes to stretch. You will be amazed at how much you do not know about stretching the body. This is especially fun with older boys. We try to have an aerobics or yoga instructor visit our varsity athletes a couple of times a year.

The key elements of stretching include the following:

- Teach your athletes how to stretch correctly.
- Implement correct stretching.
- Do not let them cheat the stretch. Implement effective strategies.
- Do not let your stretch time be chat time.

2. Organize and Plan Activity Based on Needed Skills

You are now ready to move into the core of your workout. An effective workout moves through a variety of activity, does not focus too long on a single skill set, and involves everyone.

Technique, Skill, and Drills

The technique portion of the workout is dictated by skills your athletes need to develop. Dribbling skills in soccer, blocking skills in football, base running skills in baseball and softball, and shooting skills in basketball are just a few.

Technique is a part of every workout and lasts as long as you need. You are always moving your team to better skill until they get where you want them to be in personal execution of biomechanic motion relative to the sport you coach. During the technique portion, teach the particular components of the skill, making sure that your athletes understand what they must be able to do in order to perform those skills during competition. Technique is new to us old couch potatoes. I earned a two-year athletic scholarship in college. My coach's idea of technique was running and climbing rope. We were in great shape but had a very limited understanding of the biomechanics of the sport. While attending a coaching clinic after my college career, I remember an Olympic coach say, "Now we will work on the technique of this skill." I was amazed. I had no idea that you could break down a simple movement into a dozen or more physical components. But you can, and you must.

Technique is the elements of physical motion that are specific to your sport. Teaching biomechanics to your athletes is necessary for them to improve. Technique is more critical today than ever before because other coaches are teaching it so you must too. Kids' lack of physicality means that they come to your team less capable than they used to be. You cannot assume that your 112-pound twelve-year-old has quick feet; you must develop them, which is why kids need coaches. Skills are the things required by the sport; hitting is a baseball and softball skill, running is a multi-sport skill, shots on goal are hockey and soccer skills, and passing is a football skill. Working is the key to all others skills.

The specific technique that you need to improve is directed by what is happening poorly in competition. Decide which skills need work. Clarify their technique through conversation with other coaches, your assistants, the league, mentors, whomever. Break the skill down to its smallest technical component and continuously rehearse it. For example, imagine you are coaching baseball and want to improve your defense. The problem is that your kids make bad throws to the wrong places. Set up stations—the more the better since you want to involve as many kids as possible. Let the athletes make the correct throw again and again.

Rotate the kids through each station. Add base runners to increase participation and make the drill as game-like as possible.

Game or Competition Situations

Game and competition situations are simply creating a scenario and running the drill or play redundantly, only now you are adding the time and score component that could happen in a game (for example, fourth down with twelve seconds left to play, two out and the bottom of the ninth, a one point lead and you have two shots at the free throw line). Whatever you can think of that puts the skills into a game-like condition to let your kids get used to simply executing the skill regardless of the circumstance.

Live Play

Live play is scrimmage and always comes later in practice. During live play you create as much of a game or match situation as possible while maintaining a controlled drill-type environment. You want to always engage as many athletes as possible, but during games you only play one team at a time. During practice you want as much repetition for each athlete as possible. The worst is to see a team with only a few players in motion and the rest standing. Avoid those moments as much as possible, although sometimes it cannot be helped. Scrimmage is important, but your objective is to develop everyone.

Conditioning

Conditioning makes your athletes stronger and faster. It consists of wind sprints or another fast, strenuous part of your workout. An effective workout will dedicate a portion of time to helping the athletes strengthen their muscles and cardiovascular systems. Do not neglect this time. You must continue to push their capacity for activity. You must pay close attention to your athletes. Do not be so hard on them that conditioning becomes drudgery. Do not hurt them. Ask if they are sore the next day. Soreness indicates strain, so back off if they are hurting. Always listen to them and pay attention to their physical condition. Knowing your athlete and building a good relationship with them allows you to encourage greater effort.

3. Make the Ending Fun

The number-one reason kids play a sport is to have fun, and the number-one reason they quit playing a sport is that it stops being fun. Keep the end of practice fun by playing games. Designing games that are specific to the sport is good but not always necessary. Sometimes a complete departure from the skills of the sport is necessary. For example, we take wrestlers to the swimming pool a couple of times a month to end our practice. A fun ending to practice improves your coaching. The beginning and end of a conversation are more easily remembered than the middle. The same is true of a workout. If the middle of your practice is tough, which it will be if you are making your kids better in the sport, then a fun end to practice leaves your kids smiling and ready for the next workout. As they leave, ask them if they had fun. Sweaty hair and smiling faces mean you are doing things right.

Link Their Minds with Determination

The relationship of a coach and athlete should not be taken lightly. The quality of that relationship has a direct correlation to your effectiveness as a coach. If you want to facilitate change within your athletes, they must respect you. A magical moment occurs when you help young people discover they can do more than they thought possible. This technique begins with a simple decision to push them through personal fatigue in spite of how late it may be in the game or how discouraging the score may be.

I have developed a drill that creates a relationship and honor. I adjust it accordingly, but I use it at every level of coaching. While conditioning with wind sprints, for example, I ask for one more, then one more, and then one more. I push my athletes until they are tired. I am looking for them to make a simple commitment deep enough to set their mind to the task. When someone complains, I step in front of the team and say, "I want you to step to that line ready to run one more sprint. Do not complain. Tell yourself that can do this."

Put them on the line and blow the whistle. After a couple more, they will be dragging their rear ends. Be careful not to hurt them, but also be sure to push them. You are looking for a universal commitment without telling them that that is what you want. Let them discover something within themselves. When every kid steps to the line without complaining, when every kid is locked into a set position ready to give the necessary effort, let them stay there for a moment and then say, "Good job. That's enough." As they walk away from the line, they will be tired, but you will have instilled in them a determination to do what is required. They will have completed an exercise that caused them to keep going despite their fatigue. Greater commitment will follow. You will have coached them through focusing on a single task. Tell the team, "You just decided that you will step to the task at hand. All I ask is that you outwork everyone you meet. That is all. Simply decide. You outwork them and we will be just fine." And we always are.

Young people's involvement in youth sports will transform them. As coaches we should encourage children to greater physical activity and then watch that action blossom into faith in themselves. Seeing a child grow and improve renders a rare dividend. In time, your involvement with a child can allow you the fortunate pleasure of watching his faith in himself blossom into passionate intuition, skill, and accomplishment.

10

THE GAME WITHIN THE GAME

Keep Attitudes Cool during Competition

My two sons were forever changed. They gained confidence because quitting was never an option. It is not now. They are in solid marriages and meet challenges head on. Maintaining positive attitudes holds them in a better place than many of their peers. I wanted my kids to possess a love of work, tenacity, and discipline. I did not know how to teach them. Mike did.

—*Michelle J., Mother*

THE OTHER DAY I ATTENDED my son's baseball game. The opposing team had a should-a-been assistant coach who revealed himself as the game progressed. His horrid language was pervasive, and he showed his team and the crowd a classless behavior contrary to anything that Little League baseball should be about. He questioned everything, whether a simple call, critical moment, close call on base, or a no-swing third strike. Regardless of what the umpire called, he emerged from the dugout screaming. The closer the calls came to affecting the score, the more vulgar and profane his language became. The umpire was long-suffering and appeared to have no recourse to the problem. It was, after all, Little League, and he had no help. In the stands, we watched confrontation after confrontation. The parents and onlookers were visibly uncomfortable. As the game continued and the score grew tight, this coach's players began copying his style and abusive verbiage. Things were getting out of control. The umpire made repeated attempts to set this silly sod down with no success.

Finally, the vulgar assistant coach jumped up to once again screech. Interestingly enough, he prefaced his final tirade with his own self-imposed exile. He actually said, "I'll throw myself out, but you have got to be !%@#*&* kidding me! That is the most %@#*&* call I have ever seen." He then left the game, went to his car, got on the phone, and remained there until the game was over. His team held on to win the game. Following the two teams' meeting at home plate and telling each other "good game," the coach returned to the dugout. This coach, the epitome of poor sportsmanship, surprised us all by congratulating the players on my son's team for their good play.

I think he actually believed his behavior is how a coach should act. His anger and tirades were a calculated part of the game because he believed that is what coaches do. He displayed no remorse for his behavior, offered no explanation for such poor sportsmanship, and acted as if nothing was wrong. All was forgiven. All was right. His team won, and he showed no remorse for his actions.

I found the episode appalling, unbelievable, and sad. By the end of the season, the league administrators had received enough complaints about this team and their coaches that they suspended the team from post-season play. I will leave the merits of that decision alone. Punishing players for poorly behaved coaches should always be a last resort. But what a shame it is that this coach cost a team with a winning record an opportunity to play in tournaments. I am certain that he told his team that the league's disciplinary action was not his fault. The administration obviously was doing his team wrong. What twisted message did his players receive?

Your Sideline Role

I detest the philosophy of the aforementioned coach. I hope he is a rare exception for what happens in the name of coaching. I trust your sideline conduct is nothing like his. In fact, I know you are not like him because you are open to new thinking. He is not. What do you do to manage the game while improving your program?

The Chess Match

A sporting event consists of two parts—the physical and the mental. The physical components consist of movement, athleticism, and the ability to conform physicality to the needs of the game. The mental component consists of the intellectual chess match that accompanies the game. As a coach you must build both parts. Neglecting one affects the other. Discussing complex game plans and blocking assignments with a Little League football team is fine if the intellectual maturity of your team can sustain those conversations, but you cannot coach what they cannot do.

I watched a football coach spend 90 percent of his practice time running and learning hundreds of plays at the expense of conditioning, blocking, tackling, stretching, foot speed, hip strength, and all of the other elements needed to develop young players. I was his assistant, and more than once he stopped my conditioning, skills, and technique development or stretching so he could run plays. It was fun for the backs and ends but drudgery for everyone else. It is easy to spend more time on the chess game than on the physical game because it is probably what you best know, or at least it is what you believe you know. But when you get into competition, you will always be defeated by the action of the sport itself until you develop players who can play and athletes who are in sufficient condition to stay in the game for as long as needed. While I acknowledge that exceptions exist, who can forget Boise State stuffing Oklahoma in a football bowl game with a last second trick play a few years ago? You are best served by equally yoking the development of mind and body.

Three Simple Secrets

Three simple secrets for managing the intellectual game within the physical one are improvement happens in practice, competition measures skill, and never articulate outcomes.

1. Improvement Happens in Practice

Athletes get better during practice. More physical development takes place during rehearsal than in games. By building capacity and independence for each member of your team, you become a stronger unit within your sport.

I once coached a talented receiver. He was a good size and had great hands, but he took his eyes off the ball as he looked downfield and dropped passes. A poor coach would stand on the sideline and roll his eyes or show some other manner of disappointment. When this receiver was younger, more often than not he was clear for the game-winning reception, only to drop it. We never criticized his drops but made time during practice for him to improve his catching. We did it by breaking down the components of the physical skill. We taught him to catch the ball at the apex of the throw and to keep his hands in a strong place. We taught him to look the ball into his hands. But we did more than talk about it; we drilled those techniques again and again. He caught hundreds of catches during practice. When he dropped passes, we always tried to boost his confidence by pointing out his improvement and reassuring him that he would catch the next one. During the six years that I coached him, he got better and better and grew taller. In his final Little League game before high school, I sent him in on defense during the final moments of the championship game. He had already caught two touchdown passes to give us the lead. We were defending a final drive as the fourth quarter seconds ticked down. He intercepted a pass using his well-groomed skills, and we won the championship. I remember thinking as I saw the ball go in his direction that the game was over. I was as confident as he was that he would catch the ball.

He would not have been successful in that moment if his physical skills had not become second nature. Had we criticized or expressed personal disappointment during his development, he would have lacked confidence at the very moment when we needed his skill.

What you do in practice is more important than what happens during a game. The concept holds true for every sport. Break down the motion. Teach the physical skills through repetition. Take the time during practice to develop physicality. It will bear fruit for your program and your athlete's future.

2. Competition Measures Skill

I have been a high school wrestling official for more than twenty-five years. A wrestling match takes place in a close environment. Within the immediate vicinity of a twenty-eight-foot circle is an official, two combatants, as many as four coaches, and a scorekeeper's table. The coaches who shout instructions during the event are usually the least effective. Quiet coaches spend their energy preparing the athlete for the competition. They are content to let the athlete perform, assess what takes place, and work on improving during the next practice. There is a time to communicate energy and support by being vocal, and there is a time to fight for your athlete when an umpire's call is incorrect or a coaching error occurs. But shouting directions in the moment of competition is a limiting behavior. Physicality is a muscle memory issue, and no amount of talking can correct it.

I learned this lesson while coaching Little League baseball. A very simple skill is for an outfielder to catch the ball using both hands. As easy as that sounds, it is difficult to coach. Kids think it is cool to catch with one hand. Some think the glove will do the work or their coach will let them get away with lazy skills. I guarantee that you will have players drop balls if you do not work on this skill.

When someone drops the ball during a game and creates the third out, the coach's immediate impulse may be to shout, "How could she miss that? The ball hit the mitt and bounced out." Yelling changes nothing for two reasons; the kid hardly hears you, and the physical nature of the skill was not addressed.

3. *Never Articulate Outcomes*

I cannot even begin to tell you the number of times I hear this:

- Don't strike out. (They strike out.)
- Don't drop the ball. (They drop the ball.)
- Don't get pinned. (They get pinned.)
- Don't give up a big play. (They give up the big play.)
- Do not let them score a goal. (They let them score a goal.)

Often when a particular outcome is articulated, it immediately comes true. Test it for yourself. Watch a game and listen to what parents and coaches say to the athletes. You will be amazed at how often someone says not to do something and a young athlete immediately does that exact thing. I believe that a coach should never articulate an outcome. Instead, the coach should speak directly to athletes in these three ways:

- Encourage before or after the moment, NEVER during it.

- Use positive, nonspecific encouragement. For example, say, "Good effort, just like practice work hard, outwork them."
- Focus on the skills of the moment rather than their outcome. For example, say, "Keep your feet moving, head up, hips low, watch the ball to the glove."

The drama of competition is created by a collision between the score and the remainder of the contesting period. When you remove the game situation, the athletic competition becomes a simple execution of skill. The game situation—how much time is left, the score, who has the ball—makes the competition interesting to watch. When the outcome of the game is on the line or a specific performance is needed to create a win, the young athlete feels immense pressure. When coaches or parents articulate outcome, they increase the pressure that kids already feel. Change that. By focusing on the skill rather than the situation, you relax the pressure. Success is more probable when your athlete is able to focus on what they have successfully done many times in practice. The task is then to merely execute the skill and forget the situation.

Having a vision for your work and a simple statement that articulates that vision is a powerful way to strengthen your team's purpose. One year a team captain shared the motto "Find a Way" with our team. It became a rallying cry that drove us through a number of difficult competitions that ended in one of our most successful seasons ever. These mottoes are important, and the best ones come from the context of your team and the personalities of your players. Look for moments when something extraordinary takes place and let that become your rallying cry.

11

DAN GABLE IS RIGHT

A Message to Parents

With special thanks to Dr. Robert Schluter, Professor of Physics at MIT and Northwestern University (ret.) and Leo Kocher, Head Wrestling Coach at the University of Chicago.

Children are a challenge in the best of circumstances. I knew to keep them busy. What I did not expect was how much influence a coach who teaches more than the game can have. Life skills last far beyond seasons. My kids know how to work hard, continue after disappointment, overcome adversity and handle hard things. You won't find that on a scorecard.

—Ann J., Mother

While presenting my Coaches Training Program, Championship Access, to a conference of high school coaches in California, I had the honor to visit with Dan Gable. He is America's great Olympian, coach, and educator. At the end of a long day of teaching, training, and demonstrating the skills of wrestling to coaches, Coach Gable stopped by my booth and told me, "Wrestling is not for everybody, but it should be."

The more I watch the challenges that our young people face, the more I see that their lack of commitment to leaving home for marriage or career is reaching epidemic proportion. As a wrestling coach of twenty years, I can point to many young men who are excelling in their personal lives because they were wrestlers. Wrestling is the most physically and psychologically grueling of sports. It is defined by effort and mental and emotional discipline, and is unflinching in its feedback. The one-on-one combative nature of the sport and the unavoidable exhaustion experienced during workouts and competitive matches combine to shine the brightest of spotlights on personal character.

No other sport reflects such a powerful correlation between work and success. Size, speed, strength, and athleticism are God-given talents. Yet, every high school in America is filled with talented athletes who lack the courage to wrestle, for wrestling is individual in nature. There is no team performance to mix with, no slacking performance to place blame upon, no one but self to celebrate victory or grieve through defeat. Wrestling is liberating because it is the most fair. Personal work ethic is paramount, and success for athletes regardless of size is possible. In team sports, especially football and basketball, natural athleticism, size, and speed take precedence when determining team members. In wrestling, diligence, effort, and tenacity create a place for any athlete willing to commit to the process and not cease trying.

Ultimately, there is no loss in wrestling. The only way a wrestler loses is to quit by removing himself from practice. Every coach knows wrestlers who reach astounding success through sheer force of will, who achieve success beyond their natural ability.

Wrestling guarantees opportunity for personal victory but also physical exertion, extreme fatigue, and humility. Yet thousands of athletes stay with it through high school, college, and beyond. Why?

Wrestlers find a deep significance in how the experience defines them. When an athlete musters the self-control required to practice every day, the endurance to last the entire season, the strength of will to finish every practice and match, the integrity to engage in battle and the courage to put his win/loss record on the line every time he steps on the mat, he discovers something very valuable about himself: he is much more than the score of the match, the outcome of a call, or the result of a battle. As my friend Coach Kocher points out, wrestlers love wrestling because of what it reveals to them about themselves. No other sport mirrors life like wrestling. No game is experienced as personally as a wrestling match. Few sports can reach so deep into the soul of its competitors and return personal worth.

There is not much glory in wrestling, but there is much gain. Wrestlers replace weak bodies with strong ones, trade insecurity with courage, and exchange anger for honor. Wrestlers have shown me courage, humility, tenacity, and bravery. Wrestling is a teacher and sometimes her lessons are harsh. When we step to the line for battle knowing that we can be defeated, the message to self in victory is easily apparent and glorious to enjoy.

But when we seek victory and are handed defeat, we are privately taught that both extremes—the ecstasy and the agony—are contrasting mirrors of the same reflection. For without risk we can never know glory. Without defeat we will never understand humility. Integrity requires that the lessons of manhood be seared on our souls by the furnace of consequence, and wrestling creates consequence every day.

At any time and at every level, a wrestler's match, tournament, or season might end in a way other than the one intended. None of us are alone or independent in that experience. Every coach has experienced the emotions of goals unmet or victories unclaimed. As painful and discouraging as these moments are, we are better people for having worked through those events, because nothing of value comes without cost—not career, family, or personal relationships.

Overcoming adversity in all of life's arenas is wrestling. Everyone who wrestles in junior high and high school achieves more than they thought possible and becomes greater through effort and discipline than they were before beginning the journey.

Everyone truly engaged in any passionate endeavor does so at personal risk that gets overshadowed by development benefits that can last the rest of their lives. When I watch young wrestlers who are not yet able to see the value of the lessons they are learning, I ask that they remember the words of Thomas Paine: "Heaven knows how to price its goods."[1]

1 Thomas Paine, Thomas Paine's Common Sense: The Call to Independence (Woodbury: New York, 1776).

Heavenly goods such as work, persistence, humor, and the thousand other emotions wrestlers feel while wrestling are divine gifts that intimately belong to the person who earned them. Character does not come easily because the qualities of integrity and self-assurance must be anchored in our lives. Young people who wrestle and experience the lessons taught by this great sport become good husbands and wives, compassionate fathers and mothers, successful professionals, and effective citizens. They are also in the best physical condition of their lives, reach home tired at night, and share this common experience with quality teammates. That is why I love wrestling.

12

FIVE MEASURES OF A QUALITY YOUTH SPORTS PROGRAM

Choosing Your Teams, Leagues, or Coaches

I've coached with Mike and am a huge fan. I absorbed everything he taught me and it works. Do it right, stay healthy, prepare, and good things will happen. I took poor teams and made them better and good teams and made them great.

—*Bart R., Little League and High School Football Coach*

I RECENTLY STOOD BEHIND THE dugout and watched a Little League baseball game. A young athlete committed an error, something that happens all the time, but this mistake allowed the game-winning run to score. She dropped a fly ball. What appeared to be a routine catch hit her glove and tumbled to the ground. When the inning was over, the coach met her at the third baseline and unloaded his frustration. Yelling, screaming, and red-faced intensity greeted a child who missed a fly ball during a Little League game.

The angry coach is not the remarkable revelation of this moment. Most coaches keep their calm, and verbal abuse is never justified. He was making a more critical error than she, but it was her reaction that astounded me. The player looked at the coach, waited for him to finish, and then walked to the team bench and sat down.

I then heard a most unbelievable dialog between two Little League players.

A second player commented, "Wow, Coach was ticked."

The scolded player looked at her friend and simply replied, "What?"

During the moment of reprimand, when the coach was upset and embarrassing himself, this child turned off his noise. The waiting drink of water at the team bench carried more meaning for her than the coach's intended instruction. This young player shut him out so successfully that she failed to notice his anger, even though her teammate and I worried for her well-being.

I was astounded because I still reel from Little League mistakes that I made. Even though I never had a coach effectively teach me how to handle errors or defeat, I would have been devastated by a coach getting upset with me.

How this child was affected is yet to be seen, but the surprising element of the moment for me was her reaction. It was another indication of the way that today's child is different than we were, and we must coach them in new ways in order to be effective. Here was a child so accomplished at shutting out noise that she simply flipped a switch and turned off this unpleasant encounter. I started thinking of all the ways that our children differ and how that difference impacts the youth sports experience.

Let me suggest five measures to create a successful Little League team, regardless of the sport.

1. *Encourage and Allow Play for Fun's Sake*

While watching my boys compete in a wrestling tournament, I saw an unusual sign on the wall of a local high school gymnasium: "No Unsupervised Play."

A number of factors are at work here. We over-schedule our children and leave them little free time. We deny creative play. We fear for their safety, and it's often difficult to find safe places that don't require adult supervision. The threat of injury and litigation makes schools, churches, and neighborhood open spaces unavailable. Video games, computers, texting, and other electronic devices compete for their attention. Unfortunately, today's young athlete usually only engages in sports under adult supervision. Sandlot baseball and pickup basketball games are disappearing faster than analog televisions. As a Little League coach, your job is to make sports fun and feel like playtime.

2. *Design Workouts That Engage Every Child*

Every child is different. Working with a dozen kids with a single plan is problematic. Coaches must be flexible to meet the needs of children with attention deficit disorder or other challenges. Parents can quickly blame a child's lack of enjoyment on the coach's absence of skill. A workout must be designed to embrace every child, regardless of physical or emotional levels.

3. *Teach and Expect Work*

A young person who stays on task and can work for an extended period of time is the exception rather than the rule. A young athlete's capacity for work comes from the quality of coaching rather than from the child. Coaches cannot assume that a child knows how to work. You must teach the child how to work and expect him to do it.

4. *Reject Quick Fixes and Easy Solutions*

Our culture promotes instant fame, quick cash, and an "everyone gets in for free" mentality. This does not work in sports. Acquiring an athletic skill takes time and effort. Do you teach the development of skills, knowing that most kids will miss kicks, drop passes, or fall short thousands of times before becoming athletically excellent?

5. *Define Winning*

Youth sport programs give children a laboratory to investigate life's experience. Through youth sports, children develop more than physicality; they learn social skills that allow them to work with others, personally experience the value of working toward a simple goal, undergo loss while staying connected to personal issues of character and honor, learn the disappearing art of winning with class or losing with grace, and understand the importance of being active now and for the rest of their lives. No one disagrees that these are important issues. The coach and program are the guardians of the gate, the keepers of the keys, the dispensers of wisdom and insight.

The coach is not just the guy or gal who yells when things go wrong. I suggest that it is a new day and those of us engaged in the mentoring and coaching of young people need to look for solutions other than the ones we experienced when we were in Little League.

The challenge for every parent with a child involved in Little League sports or a coach of young athletes is to admit that the book for the new school of coaching is just being written. There is great danger in assumption and nothing more dangerous than assuming that the neighborhood Little League program has its act together. If you take for granted that the youth sports program you just signed up for is going to develop your children in the way that you have in mind, you may be sorely disappointed. Your first impression of the kind-hearted person willing to coach is no indication that they have the skill, desire, or vision to leave your child better at the end of the season than at the beginning.

Get involved, volunteer, ask questions, and be a solution.

13

FIVE THINGS EVERY PARENT AND COACH MUST UNDERSTAND

You Chill on the Sidelines

> The roots of everything that I am today—hard worker, dedicated family man, service oriented person—is traced to my time in this program. My parents' divorce shook my confidence to the core. I was twelve at the time. Any sense of security that I had as a teenager I received from my athletic experiences. Coach Mike was not my father. To this day he still is my friend.
>
> —*Leroy J., Information Systems Sales Professional*

Plato, the famous Greek philosopher, said that the beginning is the most important part of any work. It was true for Plato and his students nearly 2500 hundred years ago, and it is true for our children today.

During a recent baseball game, I watched a sixteen-year-old boy hit a home run. A nearby parent mentioned how well the young man hit the ball.

You should have seen him when he was eight, I thought. As his Little League coach for two seasons, I watched him pick more dandelions than he ever hit baseballs. But who he was then and who he is now are separate people. He is different today due to maturity, growth, strength, and skill, yet he remains the same good young man that his mother sent to the ball field eight years ago.

Youth Sports Can Be Good or Bad

The youth sports experience can be good, as was the case of my home run hitter. Or it can be bad, as was the case of every eight-year-old who was not encouraged, did not learn to love the game, or never found approval from the coach or acceptance from the team. If we disregard the import of underpinnings, we cannot be surprised when our kids are less capable and discouraged by the entire Little League experience. From the moment we start coaching a youth team or enroll our own child in Little League, until those wonderful moments years later when we watch them as accomplished athletes or successful adults, the relationship between mentors and Little League athletes will be a distinctive one. The glorious relationship between parents, coaches, and athletes can be improved in today's coaching environment when you recognize five important things.

1. Yesterday's Coaching Styles Are Old News

We must talk to athletes today differently than we were spoken to back in the day. Today's child is bombarded with so many messages and so much information that they become skilled at tuning out anything that they don't want to hear. We program them to be able to change channels and disregard what fails to interest them. My youngest grandchild knows how to quickly push a button or touch a screen to trade one stream of consciousness for another. Today's child removes your actual voice just as seamlessly. If you think that screaming like your old high school coach will motivate today's children, you are wrong. Last winter at a wrestling tournament I witnessed an old-school coach letting his athlete know how poorly he thought of the kids' performance. He was direct and he was coarse. It was not an affirmation but a condemnation. There was no mistaking this coach's message. I would never speak the way he spoke. I heard that kind of coaching many years ago. I hated it then and abhor it now. Screaming is wrong on a personal level and never works on a global one.

2. *The Success of a Team Requires New Ways of Doing Things*

You must engage these new ways if you want to be an effective coach or parent of a young athlete. Not only are you working to improve their ability to play a game, but you are also engaging them emotionally and personally. Social interaction, playing with kids, engaging them in team play, and exercising their muscles and cardiovascular systems are all part of the benefits of coaching and elements of your job description. You must address these issues because they affect what happens in your team and during their games. You must learn to look for opportunities to engage and mentor children. You will find teaching moments everywhere, not just in the score of the game.

3. *The Evolution of Sports Technology Is Revolutionary*

Video is just one of the ways that technology changes coaching. I would love to see myself wrestle or play football when I was a Little Leaguer, but that video does not exist. You can use videos to show the skills of your athletes, help them improve, and watch accomplished players in action. YouTube and the Internet lets grandparents see the great plays as well. Let technology guide development and understanding of skills in a way that helps your athletes.

4. *Equipment Used Twenty Years Ago Is Laughable Today*

Safety is more assured than ever before due to improvements in equipment. Pick up an old wooden bat and hit a few pitches, and then pick up an aluminum one and swing away. Every piece of sports equipment has changed as much as titanium bats have changed from wooden ones. You must understand those changes and know today's equipment. Become a student of it. Visit stores and websites. Speak directly with well-trained sales people at quality vendors before purchasing or recommending any equipment.

5. *Sports Nutrition and What Your Children Eat Are Not the Same Things*

A sports season is a wonderful time to trade bad eating habits for good. In my Little League programs we have one night at the beginning of the season when we drink the last soda pop, eat the last candy bar, and chomp the last potato chip. I am amazed by the number of parents who tell me a few weeks into the season how much they appreciate that I gave their children a reason to eat better food. They are also appreciative of the fact that members of my teams actively accept the challenge and enthusiastically dive into appropriate nutrition as part of their participation on our team. If we don't take what our children eat more seriously, we will turn around in another generation and see our children grow even larger, more obese, and less nourished than they are today.

Obesity is far more destructive to the well-being of our children than just adding excess pounds. The danger virtually reaches every organ in an obese child's body, leading to probably irreversible damage later in life.

According to the *Washington Post*, "Doctors are seeing confirmation of this daily: boys and girls in elementary school suffering from high blood pressure, high cholesterol and painful joint conditions; a soaring incidence of type 2 diabetes, once a rarity in pediatricians' offices; even a spike in child gallstones, also once a singularly adult affliction. Minority youth are most severely affected, because so many are pushing the scales into the most dangerous territory."[1]

With one in three children in this country overweight or worse, the future health and productivity of an entire generation and a nation could be in jeopardy.

I make it part of our regime to teach children and parents what it takes to overcome eating sugar and leading sedentary lifestyles as we move into greater activity during our season. I also discuss what should be eaten on games day. Let me share six ways to help them.

1. Challenge each child to eat colors every day: red in apples, green in grapes, yellow in bananas, and so on.
2. Stop drinking soda and drink more water.
3. Eliminate energy drinks. They are dangerous.
4. Ask parents to take an inventory of daily diet and assess what each child is eating and how much.
5. Start reading food labels.
6. Become a student of nutrition.

---

1 Risa Lavizzo-Mourey and Robert Wood Johnson Foundation, "Obesity Threatens a Generation," *Washington Post*, May 17, 2008.

You can make no assumptions about where your children are in terms of their physical capacity, knowledge of the game, or ability to be part of your team. Your role as a youth coach and parent of a Little League athlete should include these recommendations and more. Little League is a continuing process, and you are just beginning.

One of the problems we face in sport is that natural gifts and talent are so decisive as to exercise undue pressure on the Little League experience. There is a reason professional teams pay big money for the best talent they can find. Remove Kobe Bryant from the Los Angeles Lakers and what do you have? Why is a first round draft pick worth millions of dollars to an NFL team?

Is Josh Beckham worth the millions the LA Galaxy is paying him? A college's ability to win an NCAA national title is based on the strength of their recruiting class. Las Vegas odds makers judge the possibility for success of every NCAA division football and basketball team by the talent of its incoming freshman. It is simple. No great freshman means no great seniors. A winning program, which is the focus of college and professional sports, will always seek the best talent. When all things are considered, more often than not, talent will make a difference at those levels. But our duty is completely different when coaching young athletes. Our responsibility is to improve every member of our team.

Motivating kids to work, try, and enjoy the process can bring you great satisfaction. Little League connects you with children who will exhibit varying levels of talent, diligence, and commitment. If you spend any time in Little League, you will one day have a talented lazy kid that you would gladly trade for a not-so-talented hard worker. We must coach them all. The kids we coach are there because their parents enrolled them. We are there to create a fun and safe place, nurture, cultivate, and discover their potential. Talent is important but is only a fragment of the picture.

In a typical Little League program such as baseball, you will have two or three talented kids out of the twelve registered for your team. All-Stars begins moving that talent and capacity into a single team. If talent and a child's ability to help you win is the only measurement you use, then prepare for failure because in Little League, talent cannot be everything. If talent is our only measurement, then we ostracize most of the kids we will coach. The difference that talent gives the naturally gifted can be offset by heart, commitment, hard work, and dedication. You can lift the less gifted athletes up by using the skills and techniques of this book and create a formidable team. Talent in sport is hug, but in Little League it is only one component. Too many coaches are lazy. They only want to cherry pick the talent and work with the athletes capable of making them look good.

Focusing on winning reinforces that attitude. High school football is becoming more and more like college football was twenty years ago; kids are recruited, enrollments and residences are changed, and coaches are lured to create winning programs in the quest for titles and championships. An athlete who works hard in the Little League program may find himself locked out in high school by the talented kid brought in to take his place in the name of winning. It is not my place to say if that is right or wrong. I like winning as much as anyone, but it is not the focus of my programs.

A coach that I respect was a member of a national championship football team while in college. When our boys and their football team won a game, he simply pointed out to the boys that winning was nothing big. It was the result of our hard work and what we expected to happen as a result of our application of skills during the game. We worked on several teams together, taking the last one to a 12–1 championship season. But our focus was not winning. It was the boys and the qualities of our program that we are discussing here. My point is to cultivate the discussion that surrounds effective coaching. Colleges and professionals must win because that is their reason for being. Little League must count winning in the new ways discussed in this book.

An Idaho Weigh-in

To the right is one of my favorite pictures from the Little League days with my two sons. We were visiting my brother's ranch before travelling to Pocatello, Idaho, to compete in the Western Regional Wrestling Championships. As part or our preparation, we had to make sure that we could meet the correct weight in order to enter the tournament. We were ninety minutes away from the Idaho State University campus, where the tournament was being held. We started the day by doing farm chores, in particular moving bales of hay that weighed about a hundred pounds

each. Lifting and stacking them required great effort, and in the summer, heat creates plenty of perspiration. After a couple of hours of hard work, we needed to get on our way. I asked my brother if he had a good scale, and he said he had several, the most accurate being the one he used to weigh potatoes and animal feed. (I am not kidding.) We brought out the old scale, and the boys made their weight, entered the tournament, and enjoyed a good meal and a great night's sleep before enjoying the actual competition. We had a good time because my boys and I were working together for a common cause, and my boys were disciplining their effort and caloric intake for a few hours to hold their body weight. I could not resist getting Whalebone, my brother's old mule, out of the corral and into the shot. We did not weigh the mule.

AFTERWORD

A Beautiful Case Study

I SAT ON THE CORNER of the mat and watched as nineteen young men reached deeply into my soul and spoke to my heart of honor, dignity, truth, and hard work. It was a time most excellent.

For the past five years, while my two sons have been moving through our junior and senior high schools, I have been working with this group of young athletes. It was a journey that allowed me to test every theory that I hold dear while maintaining a relationship with my sons by investing in their experience and friends.

Two junior high schools feed into the high school that my sons would be attending. Nearly six years ago, one of the schools burned to the ground. It was a horrible accident that began in the computer room and engulfed the entire school before firemen could douse the flame. The building was a total loss, and after much deliberation regarding the various ways to maintain continuity for the students while the new school was built, the district administration decided that both schools could function independently on the same campus; two student populations would share physical space while maintaining their own cultures and faculty.

Our school district maintains an excellent intramural sports program for the fourteen junior high schools, including school sponsored wrestling teams. I had committed to coach one of the junior high teams for four years while my sons moved through the program. The fire changed my plans and created an opportunity for our wrestling program. I told the two principals that I would be happy to coach both teams. Because we only had one mat and a single workout facility that we were compelled to share between the two schools, it was a simple conversation. In fact, the junior high school administrators thought I was doing them a favor. It was I who was gaining from the experience because I could have all the boys under my direction during the all-important junior high development years.

In point of fact, I was establishing a training ground to build the later varsity experience upon. I was once told that in Russia, the best coaches work with the youngest athletes. I do not know if that is true, but I believe it should be. The beginning of any work is the most critical. When you work with young athletes, the foundational strengths required for competitive success is so important that bad technical athleticism allowed during the foundational time is difficult, if not impossible, to correct later.

By putting all of the boys in one place, I could oversee those important formative workouts. I could apply what I had been learning for more than two decades and create vision, establish technique, and instill a love for the sport and hard work. I wanted to groom all of the athletes during these important foundational years. My ulterior motive was to make as great an impact as I could on the team that I planned to follow through their high school careers. Because I had been involved at all levels of our program, I had seen kids come out of the junior high with such poor technique, work ethic, and commitment to the sport that they never had a fair chance to reach their own potentials. Overcoming a poor beginning is difficult, if not impossible. Having all of the boys under my direction was a great blessing. It freed the principals of one less integration problem, leaving their time frames open to deal with the many logistical details of mixing two schools on one campus. While each school remained the same, we became a team. While developing this team, I saw firsthand the great power that comes when you create a clear and precise vision of what may be possible in the future. I often told this team who they could become if we kept working, supporting one another, and holding to a cause greater than ourselves. I learned that during adversity it is the commitment to possibility, the shared understanding of vision, that sustains. I saw it take hold in my athletes. I knew it was an experience that could point to greater potentials and success in the future. Each of us needs to have the ability to create vision and hold to dreams in our lives, education, and personal relationships.

Our two junior highs schools were named Churchill and Wasatch. In an effort to converge the two cultures, we called ourselves Chursatch, then Washill, and finally Skyline Junior High. As part of my team building and vision mapping process, I created a sign that simply read, "Through these doors pass the best wrestlers in the history of Skyline High School." I hung it above the entrance of our workout room. Fast forward through hundreds of workouts, dozens of matches, and five years of experience while we grew in physical stature and technical ability. The young men from my two junior high schools were now the varsity wrestling team in our high school. When we moved to the varsity level, I took the sign with me.

Our high school was very successful both in athletics and academics. Football was king, and while our wrestling program has generated many tough wrestlers, including our fair share of region and state individual champions, we had never won a team wrestling championship during an official state high school tournament. This team, created as a result of my application of theory and principle, was about to make history.

This was my last tournament for the high school where I raised my children. I have been in the corner of every state or region championship wrestling match that our school and our athletes have competed in. Much of what I have learned about young athletes has begun and been tested in our wrestling room. Many times I have taken the things that I learn from this ancient sport and apply them with great success to improve baseball players' ability to maintain a stance through a baseball swing, a throw, or while fielding; I have seen football players gain greater balance during the hand to hand battle of blocking and tackling, and seen the success generated by quick feet and great hip position in order to hold strength during every play. I have watched the capacity of basketball players develop because strong core and hips allowed them to drop low while sustaining defensive positions. All of these skills open doors to greater physicality that is required to groom and develop young athletes. I am an observer. My quest for understanding began in my own struggles as well as other coaches'. I sought solutions. I listened. I questioned. I was not held captive to former coaching paradigms and always accepted the counsel of wise experience. My coaching laboratory was about to return huge dividends on my investment.

We entered the championship tournament having defeated every other team during the regular season dual team matches. A tournament has a very different scoring system. Having strength in one area does not always translate to success in the other. I liked our chances, but in wrestling, as in every other sport, you must ultimately have the competition. You can say what you want, write what you will, but only competition delivers results. I was about to witness the principles of individual responsibility, hard work, good training, and intelligent coaching contained in this writing and evident in my athletes through many years of hard work.

For this year's championships, we were using a different scorekeeping process than we had used in previous years. In wrestling, the results of each match creates points. Every member of the team contributes. An individual championship, or first place in any weight, creates the most points. Wins for third and fifth places are especially crucial because they represent the final opportunity to score advancement points. Every point matters, but a win during the final matches of the tournament earns place points in addition to points for the margin of victory. In years past we could enter two athletes at each of fourteen weights and combine the earned points of both athletes. This year we decided to still enter two athletes but only score one. The team generating the most points would still be crowned champion, but this new way of running the tournament was not supported by the host school's computer program. We could not keep a running tournament score. When the first of two days of competition ended, we did not know the score. We could, however, manually count the match points and results. Because we were doing well, and because I felt that we were actually capable of winning this region championship, I started counting the points myself.

At the beginning of the second day, we had nineteen boys left in the competition, and by my count we were leading the tournament by a single point. Our strongest wrestlers were in the final matches to be held at the end of the competition. But if we were to win, it would be because of the performance of our second and third level competitors. It was imperative that they keep winning through the consolation competition. The longer a wrestler stays in the tournament, the more points they contribute. Following each round, members of my team would ask about the score. Because the score that I was keeping was unofficial, I kept saying that we were close or I liked our chances. I never gave them numbers because I was not sure that my scores were correct. They were as close as I could figure them, but we would not officially know until after all of the matches were wrestled at the end of the night.

As the day progressed, an incredible thing began to unfold. Every boy on the team contributed. Every boy gave his best. Every boy moved through the portal of growth that leads to a greater level of maturity. I saw them accept responsibility for the day, shoulder the workload that was before them, work endlessly, never stop trying, and exult with each other through every victory. Round by round we increased our lead. More important than that, round by round our preparation for this day became apparent. We pinned matches we should have won. We won matches we had no reason to win. Losses that could have been major were minor. On and on we worked. The medals matches are the last round of competition before the finals. There are two matches at each weight and twenty-eight matches in all. A win at this time in the tournament is huge because you are competing for either third or fifth. The championship matches for first place are to follow.

We had fourteen boys wrestling in this round on three mats with another five who would wrestle in the championship finals. I sat in the coach's corner of the middle mat and watched as we won eleven of those fourteen matches. Every one of those boys rose to their own levels of excellence by contributing victories. We finally put the score out of reach from our competition during those matches. We won the tournament because of those final wins by our second and third level athletes. Many of those athletes were tremendous success stories because they were there because of work, diligence, team allegiance, and more. Later that night it became official. We were the high school region champions for the first time in the history of our school. During our next workout, I pointed to the worn out, ragged sign above the entrance to our workout room: "Through these doors pass the best wrestlers in the history of Skyline High School." Indeed, they were.

At the end-of-season banquet, my wrestlers gave me a sheet of paper with their personal comments on it. Here is a sampling of what they said:

- "Thanks for never giving up on me."—Paul G.
- "Thanks for making this program great and for letting me be part of it."—McKay R.
- "Thanks for all you have done for me, on and off the mat. You have helped me get past my struggles due to the lessons you have taught me. Thanks for understanding and helping me improve.

Thanks for the hours of help for the past four years. I will make you proud."—Hunter W.

- "You are probably the most fun coach ever."—Kevin T.
- "You've got the lessons of life figured out."—Derek J.
- "Thank you so much for everything, you have made a huge difference for me. I am so glad that I was able to have you as a coach."—Garrett B.

And finally, the finest compliment I ever received from the parent of an athlete:

> The opportunities in life to be touched by extraordinary concepts are few. Our son blossomed and grew under Michael Clapier and his coaching philosophy. Lessons learned and character built under Michael's watchful care will bless our family for a lifetime. We cannot say thank you enough.
>
> —Kim Brunnenmeyer, Father

As much as I love trophies for winning and accolades for training champions, I love creating results like these. My team is on the page to the right. I am on the far right.

In a world fervently seeking rights of passage for our young people, the methods discussed in this book will effectively teach the components of life that will matter not for a season but for a lifetime. Coaches, parents, and youth leaders who can take the activity of the moment and elevate it from a task at hand to communication skills are to be admired. Leading young people through positive physical activity into personal responsibility and life skills is more than a space filler; they enter into the realm of mentor, tutor, and life-changing friend whose influence becomes timeless.

ABOUT THE AUTHOR

Michael Clapier is a parent, grandparent, coach, and mentor for parents and coaches. His study of Little League sports and children is a continuing process that began more than twenty-five years ago.

His passion is studying the physical and personal development of children through baseball, softball, track and field, wrestling, cross country, and basketball. He has seen what works and knows how to create more than mere fun in a Little League team. He knows how to affect, teach, and influence young people throughout their lifetime.

His service to youth includes Boy Scouts of America for nearly thirty years and church youth groups in the United States and in Canada even longer. Clapier is the 2016 National Secondary (High School) Assistant Coach of the Year present by the NWCA, National Wrestling Coaches Association, the governing body for coaches on collegiate and secondary levels.

SCAN TO VISIT

WWW.CLAPIERSPEAKS.COM